Inspiring Young Minds

INSPIRING YOUNG MINDS

Scientific Inquiry in the Early Years

Julie Smart, PhD

Redleaf Press®
www.redleafpress.org
800-423-8309

Published by Redleaf Press
10 Yorkton Court
St. Paul, MN 55117
www.redleafpress.org

First edition 2017
Cover design by Amy Fastenau
Cover photograph by Brian Bray/iStock
Interior design by Erin Kirk New
Typeset in Berkeley Oldstyle Medium
Interior photos by Julie Smart, except on page 25 by Nurjani/iStock
    and page 81 by Christopher Futcher/iStock
Printed in the United States of America
24 23 22 21 20 19 18 17   1 2 3 4 5 6 7 8

Library of Congress Cataloging-in-Publication Data
CIP data is on file with the Library of Congress

Printed on acid-free paper

FSC
www.fsc.org
MIX
Paper from
responsible sources
FSC® C011935

To my Irish twins, Drew and Claire,

for inspiring me with their endless curiosity

and for allowing me to see the world anew

through their eyes.

Table of Contents

Acknowledgments

I would like to thank the many people who have offered their love and support throughout the process of developing this book. Many thanks to Redleaf Press for believing in this first-time book author and especially to Kara Lomen and Laurie Herrmann for guiding me through the incredible journey of publishing my first book. Thank you to my editor, Kari Cornell, for working with me through many rounds of careful edits to develop this book into its current form.

I could never have completed this book without the love and support of my amazing husband, Andrew; you are a constant source of encouragement and inspiration, and I am so blessed to have you in my life. Thank you to my sweet children for teaching me so much as we experience the world together and for always "doing science" with Mommy! Much love to my wonderful parents, who have stood by me from the very beginning and have given me the foundation to pursue dreams like this one!

I want to thank all of my former students, from elementary to college, for giving me the opportunity to teach science and to learn from you as we walked through many lessons, projects, and classes together. I have been honored to watch my former students go on to have students of their own and spread their love for science into the next generation. I also want to thank my mentor and colleague Jeff Marshall for helping me to grow as a science educator and researcher and for always having my best interest at heart.

There are so many other family members, friends, and colleagues who have been part of my journey to write this book. To all of you, thank you for loving me, inspiring me, keeping me grounded, and walking with me through the ups and downs of life. I love you all.

Introduction

 Inquiring Minds Want to Know . . . at 2:00 a.m.

I woke up at 2:00 a.m. one night with a three-year-old staring at me in the dark with eyes wide. As I tried to remember where I was and get my bearings, my son asked with enthusiasm, "Mommy, where do the garbage men take our garbage when they leave our house?" After realizing that I wasn't having some sort of bizarre dream, I tried to piece together a semicoherent explanation involving landfills and recycling. But my son was relentless and apparently a lot more awake than I was. He asked again, "But Mommy, where does the garbage *go*?"

This "need to know" in the middle of the night awakened me—in more ways than one—to just how many questions young children have about the world they live in. The next morning, I attempted a more thorough explanation of the journey our garbage takes once it leaves our front yard, but my son wasn't satisfied. We even tried some YouTube clips of landfills and recycling centers but to no avail. My three-year-old was going to need to see this with his own eyes in order to process the answer to his 2:00 a.m. question in his own way.

It was experiences like this that led me to write this book. I have been an educator for more than a decade and have taught inquiry-based science to early childhood students, elementary students, undergraduate education students, and K–12 teachers. Having children of my own opened my eyes to the wonder of exploring science with young children; their fervor and inquisitive nature are unmatched. I made it my mission not only to record my own children's science-related questions about the world but to plan experiences designed to guide them to the answers they so desperately wanted. This book is a collection of my adventures as a teacher and a mom, drawn from the work I've done over the past decade to engage young children in meaningful science experiences.

Where to Begin

Science explorations often begin with a single question. Sometimes it's the adult who poses the question, attempting to spark interest in something we see that children might not notice as special without our guidance (such as frogs hiding in the rocks of a pool). But sometimes—and these are the really awesome times—the questions come directly from our children; that's where *true* inquiry begins. We live in a society that is quickly losing the wonder of the unanswered question. Children are rapidly learning that when they have a question, we should "Google it." Yes, this stems from the technological society in which they are growing up, and yes, children need to learn those skills of effectively seeking information online from valid sources. But sometimes this "Google culture" in which we live makes us lazy. We get lazy about using our *own* brains—remember that gray mass between our ears?

I jokingly call my iPhone my second brain, because if an event isn't recorded in my iPhone calendar, with multiple alerts set to remind me, that event basically doesn't exist. As my dependency on my iPhone as a second brain has grown and grown, I've found that my *real* brain is less capable of remembering things. Or maybe my brain is just like a muscle that loses tone and strength when it hasn't been used frequently enough. In the same way, our children's brains will not grow to truly understand how to "do" science if we are simply plugging questions into a search engine. I want our children to learn the joy of the journey. A significant part of this joy results from doing the actual thinking required to come up with solutions.

Recently, over breakfast, my daughter asked me a simple question: "How long does it take a seed to grow into a plant?" It would have been pretty easy to put my coffee down, grab my iPhone, and look up the question on

Google. I'm sure we would have found an answer, and it probably would have been a fairly accurate one. We might have even found a YouTube video with a time-lapse sequence of a seed sprouting. But we wouldn't have gotten our hands dirty. We wouldn't have actually experienced the journey of planting a seed and taking care of it, and the excitement we felt when the seedling finally poked through the soil. So instead we planted the seed. The resulting project forms the basis for chapter 8 along with a discussion on how to help young children represent data in developmentally appropriate ways.

I have spent the past decade studying inquiry-based science instruction in K–12 classrooms and with my own young children, and I am here to tell you that it works! When I say "it works," I mean that this approach results in meaningful learning for children and helps foster a lifelong love of science. It's not always easy, but it's worth the effort. I hope that this book will help you break the process into small pieces and work on one aspect of your practice at a time. Support from the community and peers is valuable when planning and implementing inquiry-based instruction. I encourage you to enlist some of your teaching colleagues to take this journey with you. Share information and learn from each other.

And know that I am here to support you every step of the way. I can assure you I have been in your shoes and truly understand the challenges you face as a teacher every day. I thank you for the endless amount of time and energy you devote to your class, and I applaud the difference you make in the lives of the children. I invite you to share your experiences or questions as you begin to implement inquiry-based instruction in your classroom. I would love to hear from you!

So without further ado, I welcome you to the intriguing, messy, sometimes unpredictable world of inquiry. I promise there will not be a dull moment!

CHAPTER ONE
Inquiring Minds Want to Know

What are the main elements of inquiry-based instruction?

Children are natural explorers. If we allow them to do so, they will instinctively seek out the most engaging and interesting routes. The challenge as an adult is to stand back and let them flounder around in the science they are exploring. We desperately want to show them the "right answer" or tell them why something works or doesn't. But according to research, that is not how young children learn science best (Marshall and Alston 2014). There are decades of studies in education specifically on the topic of exploration in science, a method of teaching generally referred to as inquiry. What is inquiry? One of the central components of this instructional method is allowing children to actively explore a scientific concept before it is explained fully. But opponents of this method claim that children need more guidance than inquiry provides. They believe that it's better to give explicit instruction in the scientific concepts we want the children to learn and then offer activities that confirm this new knowledge. But the research supports the inquiry method (Marzano, Pickering, and Pollock 2001).

One of the most common misconceptions about inquiry-based instruction is that there is only one way to do it: we must throw our children into a room full of unfamiliar scientific materials, let them explore, and check back in a few hours. This is absolutely not the approach I'm advocating in this book. Instead, I will spell out an approach known as guided inquiry, a scaffolded, methodical technique for guiding children toward a conceptual understanding of science. Understand that by using this approach, we are not aiming for just a few right answers on a test; instead our goal is to provide children with a true, meaningful understanding of the world around them and how it relates throughout their lives. We're aiming to foster lifelong learners who can realize the excitement and wonder inherent in the natural world around them. Best of all, this approach gives children the opportunity to be an active, valued part of the learning process. That's what guided inquiry means to me, and after you've read this book, that is what I hope it will mean to you as well.

What are the main elements of inquiry-based instruction?

The inquiry model that forms the foundation of everything you will read in this book is called the 4Ex2 model (Marshall, Horton, and Smart 2009). The model is akin to the 5E model that many of you may be familiar with (Engage, Explore, Explain, Extend, Evaluate). In the 4Ex2 model, however, the evaluation process is very different. Rather than acting as a summary

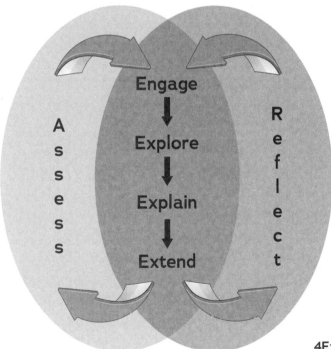

4Ex2 Instructional Model

as it does in the 5E model, in the 4Ex2 model evaluation takes place many times throughout instruction. Yes, we're talking about an intensive focus on formative assessment. Research shows that by continually evaluating student understanding during instruction and then adjusting teaching methods accordingly, teachers can vastly improve student learning (Black et al. 2004). Chapter 7 delves into greater detail about monitoring student understanding and how we can then adjust our instruction to meet students' specific learning needs.

4Ex2 Instructional Model

The following provides a description of each phase of the 4Ex2 model of inquiry-based instruction.

Engage: During the first part of inquiry-based instruction, the focus is on assessing children's prior knowledge, uncovering misconceptions, and sparking children's interest in a topic. In some cases, the Engage is also where you may work with students to develop a scientific question to be tested later on during Explore. There are numerous formative assessments that can be used at the beginning of the lesson to assess prior knowledge; refer to appendix B for several examples of formative assessments for the Engage section that have been pulled from actual early childhood and elementary inquiry-based science lessons.

Explore: The Explore section of the lesson is where the rubber meets the road; this is where your students are going to have an opportunity to actually *do* science. Explore, also called content-embedded inquiry, unites science content and scientific processes to teach children science by inviting them to *do* science. In this section of the lesson, students often test a question, engage in an experiment, or participate in an activity that allows them to explore a scientific concept. During the experiment or activity, students generally use several of the process skills within the context of the scientific content for the lesson. For example, students may make observations, make predications, classify items, take measurements, communicate their ideas, or interpret data. By uniting content and processes in science, children take on the role of a scientist and study their world in a more meaningful and relevant way.

Explain: In this section of the lesson, the teacher's role is to help children make sense of their exploration, guiding them to the main objectives of the lesson. This is where you will help students connect the previous exploration to the main ideas and learning objectives of the lesson. One of the primary criticisms of "open inquiry" is that this part of the process is often missing, meaning students may complete an exploration but are provided with no closure. The Explain phase of guided inquiry closes this gap and supports children in understanding how an exploration of science translates into conceptual understandings of the scientific content. In this phase of the lesson, the teacher's questions help guide students to verbalize their ideas about science. In chapter 5 you will find more information about the process of asking effective questions in science. In the Explain phase of the lesson, students communicate their ideas to their teacher and their peers, and the teacher highlights and explains key scientific ideas. It is essential to include students in the explanation portion of the lesson and give them an opportunity to talk about their scientific understanding of the concept. By listening to the students' ideas and responses, teachers may assess whether students are grasping the main concepts of the lesson. If they are not, you will need to adjust the lesson to reteach key concepts or present them in a different way.

Extend: The main purpose of the Extend section of the lesson is to connect the main ideas to a real-world situation or allow children to apply them in a different context. We know that children's motivation for learning science depends greatly on their ability to see science as relevant to both their present lives and to their future. The Extend is a perfect place to drive these ideas home; important career connections can also be made during this section. In addition, students may be given the opportunity to apply their scientific knowledge to a new context, such as creating something new. Many teachers choose to create a homework assignment for the Extend portion of the lesson, asking students to find examples of the science concepts they have just studied in their own homes or neighborhoods. This assignment can serve as an excellent communication tool with parents as they can observe aspects of the science their children are learning at school.

The "2" part of the model simply means that the following components are embedded in every phase of the lesson:

Assessment: In this model, assessment includes the continual collection of both formal and informal data on student learning. We will go into greater detail on the collection and use of assessment data in chapter 7. The point to note here is that the process is critical to the students' conceptual understanding. This constant collection of this data (formative assessment) distinguishes the 4Ex2 model from other inquiry models in science, which tend to view assessment as primarily summative.

Reflection: Reflection really goes hand in hand with assessment, completing the true "formative" cycle of assessment in this model. By continually reflecting on student learning, we adjust and refine our instruction to meet our students where they are. Examples of questions that might be used to reflect on a particular lesson or phase of a lesson include the following: What did students struggle to understand today? What evidence did I see that students understand this concept? What changes do I need to make to help my students gain a better understanding of this concept? When I teach this lesson in the future, what would I revise and what would I keep the same?

The 4Ex2 model provides an important framework for planning and implementing inquiry-based instruction in your own classroom. Appendixes C, D, and E provide several complete inquiry-based lessons in each major content strand: life science, physical science, and earth science. In addition, appendix A includes two graphic planning tools for using the 4Ex2 model in your own classroom.

CHAPTER TWO
Feed Me

How do we select appropriate materials for children in science?

We all get hungry, right? I know I do. (Especially when I forget to pack my lunch and the cafeteria serves that amazing rectangular pizza . . . what *is* in that stuff that makes it so addictive anyway?) In fact, eating and food happen to be of interest to all members of the animal kingdom, not just humans. And because we all need food to survive, consuming food is one of those concepts in science that is very familiar, making it startlingly easy to connect to concrete experiences. As you might have guessed, this story involves an experience with fine dining in the animal world . . . *aviary* fine dining to be exact. And, no, I'm not describing a gourmet meal aboard a Boeing 747. We're talking bird food here.

My kindergarten students were in the middle of a unit on animal adaptations. We had spent the past few days learning about adaptations that help animals stay alive such as camouflage, mimicry, and hibernation. I was looking for a way to make a meaningful connection between animals' physical adaptations and their ability to survive in their habitat. In the past, I had taught this concept by having students study photographs of various animal habitats and then make their own hypotheses about what kind of traits animals would need to thrive in that particular environment (for example, what kind of beak would they need? What kind of feet would they need?). While this approach had been somewhat successful in the past, I always came away from the lesson feeling that the thinking required to arrive at a conceptual understanding of this idea demanded that the students "work backwards," which was a bit too abstract for my young learners. This year, I wanted to find a way to engage the class in a more active and concrete way.

I decided that we were going to try to see a habitat from a bird's point of view; my students were going to transform into tiny birds and go hunting. To allow the children to test out different types of beaks, I gathered some tools that shared the traits of some common types of bird beaks: toothpick (kingfisher), tweezers (parakeet), spoon (duck), straw (hummingbird). I wanted to use the tools as concrete representations of actual bird beak shapes. For the food, I gathered different items to represent typical foods birds eat: grubs (raisins), earthworms (gummy worms), beetles (m&m's), sunflower seeds, snails (shell pasta), fish (paperclips in a cup of water), and nectar (red Kool-Aid). These items were carefully chosen so that specific bird beaks would be able to gather some of the items but not all of them. For example, you can't easily spear an m&m with a toothpick or drink nectar with tweezers. This would allow my students to see that bird beaks were physical adaptations that allowed the bird to eat the diet available in its habitat.

These materials had to be selected to provide a clear distinction between the efficiency of specific tools (i.e., beaks) for "eating" certain types of food. If each tool were equally capable of picking up each food item, the children would not be able to arrive at the critical understanding that different physical traits affected the bird's survival capabilities. So selection of appropriate materials was critical to the success of the activity.

After selecting the materials, I had to decide how to manage them and introduce them in the lesson. I first considered the potential effectiveness of presenting my students with a "set" of all four bird-beak tools. My primary concern was that presenting all of the tools at the same time would overwhelm my students with too much information at once; as they experimented with multiple tools on various types of food, their ability to process the information in an effective way would diminish. In educational psychology, we discuss a concept called "cognitive load." Basically, the human brain is capable of processing only a set amount of information at any specific time (Kirschner, Sweller, and Clark 2006); the amount of information that the human brain can process effectively depends on a variety of factors such as age, prior experiences, and ability level. When working with young children, we know that the cognitive load of an activity needs to be small. In other words, we can't bombard young brains with large amounts of information and expect them to make sense of everything. So for this activity, I needed to find a way to diminish the cognitive load of the bird-beak activity and make sure that my students collected information at a rate that they would process well. In turn, I decided to present each tool separately and allow them to have several minutes to "hunt" with each beak.

To begin the activity, I gathered my class in a circle on the rug and told them that they were going to be birds today. I quickly assessed their prior knowledge by asking a simple question, "What kind of foods do you think birds eat?" Most of my students have grown up in a suburban environment, so their most common answers revolved around the types of birds they have seen in their neighborhoods: robins eating worms, bluebirds eating birdseed, hummingbirds drinking "red juice." I explained to them that they were going to hunt with a toothpick beak and that they could use only their beak "tool" and nothing else (i.e., no hands) to hunt for the food. I had decided to make each student a separate plate full of bird food so that they would have equal opportunities to test each item. I handed each student a toothpick and a paper cup to represent their bird stomach; I didn't want my students eating the materials, since we needed to examine them afterwards, so I had to make it clear that the food should end up in the paper cup "bird stomach" and not in their mouths! With those instructions, I sent them off to hunt!

Watching the children use their toothpicks was delightful. They quickly observed that the soft and gummy foods (such as the grubs and the worms) could be easily "eaten" with the toothpick beak, but that they were unable to pick up the harder foods (such as snails and beetles). I gave them two minutes to hunt. The length of time was an important consideration, as I wanted my students to have enough time to hunt, but not enough time to come up with some creative but unrealistic methods for obtaining the food. For example, I let the time go a little long on the hunting round with the straw tool, and two crafty kids discovered that they could work together using both of their straws to lift the fish (paperclips) out of the water. I had to explain to them that birds don't practice teamwork! While this was a creative problem-solving approach, that was not the goal of the activity. Limiting the class to a small amount of time to hunt was pragmatic and kept us more focused on the simple task at hand.

After the designated hunting period, I called the class back to the rug and had them examine the items in their paper cup that they had "eaten" with their toothpick beak. We recorded our data on a simple chart that allowed the students to tape a picture of each food item beside the beak. Even at a young age, it is productive to introduce organizational tools such as charts to help children examine the information in a visual format; this also lays the groundwork for using these tools as a normative part of "doing science" in the classroom. Since the Next Generation Science Standards stress mastery of not only science content but also science processes, it is critical to integrate multiple methods for communicating results of even simple experiments.

We then used a bubble map, a visual diagram used to organize information, to match the "toothpick beak" to pictures of real birds with similar beak shapes. This was a crucial step in the lesson because at this point we were making an important connection between the *representation* of the beak that was used in the activity and the *actual* beak that is used by real birds. Children possess the ability to make a connection between a representation of a real world object and the object itself, but often they need a bit of scaffolding to develop a clear understanding of this relationship. Providing a graphic, such as a bubble map, which visually situates the actual item beside the representation of this item, can help a child make the mental connection more clearly.

How do we select appropriate materials for children in science?

Be purposeful in your selection of materials

Selecting appropriate materials in early childhood is critical. It's no coincidence that entire courses in early childhood teacher education programs are devoted to the selection of appropriate materials for instruction. In the bird beak lesson, I spent a tremendous amount of time selecting materials that would mimic the form and function of the bird beaks that I wanted to highlight. The functions of each beak needed to be unique in order to make distinctions between the way that different types of beaks allow birds to eat different types of food. If each beak had been capable of picking up every type of food, the lesson would have been ineffective in demonstrating the relationship between the type of beak a bird has and the diet it needs to survive. I had some initial concerns about the children's fine-motor skills and their use of the tweezers, so I elected to use a slightly larger size. In addition, the types of food items selected were critical to the focus of the lesson. I chose to select foods that could conceivably represent actual foods in a bird's diet (e.g., m&m's have a hard shell like a beetle; raisins are soft like a grub; shell pasta mimics the look of a snail's shell). With any science lesson, the materials selected must support the overall learning objectives of the lesson and not be overly distracting. I chose to use only one type of candy in the activity because children are easily distracted by candy; I generally steer clear of using candy in science activities for this reason, although sometimes it is justifiable if it serves a real purpose (as did the beetle-like quality of the m&m's). Choosing purposeful materials is a critical step in planning effective science instruction with young children.

When possible, select authentic materials

Now I'm not suggesting that you go out and catch a live crocodile when studying reptiles (although I'm sure that would do wonders for student engagement!). But it is always a good idea to provide students with authentic, realistic materials when possible. I am always astonished when I go into a classroom where the students are studying the parts and functions of plants and there is not one green, living thing in the room. This is an example of a time when you could easily pluck a few flowers from your yard and study *actual* plants instead of diagrams and photographs. And parents can be really helpful in these instances. Every time we begin a new unit in science, I like to send home a note informing parents of what we will be studying with a list of some authentic materials that we need for the unit. I'm often amazed by some of the collections and unusual items parents can muster up! I once had a father bring in his collection of shark teeth when we were studying fossils; another family had a pet bird and brought it in when we were studying classification of animals. The possibilities are endless when you begin asking for help. I always take lots of photographs and videos on these occasions because then at least I have pictures to show my class when the student with the shark tooth collection moves on to the next grade.

Manage your materials mindfully

The success of a science lesson can depend on how you manage your materials during the lesson. I require undergraduates who are just learning to write lesson plans to write an entire page about how they will manage their materials during each lesson. It eventually becomes intuitive, but there is definitely a learning curve. First, I never introduce a new material without allowing my students a couple of minutes to just play with it. For example, there is no way you're going to put magnifying glasses in front of five-year-olds without them wanting to explore the object immediately. You will do much better in the long run if you don't fight the natural curiosity of children, and just let them explore any new materials before beginning the activity. I recently observed a science lesson taught by a student teacher in which she placed a tub of brightly colored plastic bugs in front of each group at least fifteen minutes *before* the children got to touch the bugs and then dealt with multiple behavior issues as the students waited. Let the kids touch the bugs and get it out of the way. Then set some firm guidelines for the remainder of the lesson about how they are to handle the bugs, and the activity will run much more smoothly. You can't overcome a child's instinct to play. Thank goodness.

Another important aspect of materials management is giving thought to how students will interact with the materials if they are working in a group. Will there be a free-for-all with the magnifying glass, or will there be an established order in which students will use the materials? Will there be roles within the groups to help give each student ownership of different materials? What safety guidelines will you establish to ensure that materials are used correctly? How will materials be given out and taken up to ensure smooth transitions? How will you clean and store your materials after each lesson? These are all questions to consider in the process of any science lesson that requires a special set of materials. Considering these issues prior to the lesson will ensure that the activity runs as smoothly as possible and that each child has equal access to the materials and resources.

CHAPTER THREE
Eggs in the Roses

How do we give children opportunities to explore science for themselves?

Last spring as I was watering my plants on the patio at our home, I realized that my rose bush was filled with leaves and twigs. As I reached down to "clean it out," a bird flew out and nearly scared me to death. After I recovered from my close encounter with nature, I realized a wren had built a nest in my rose bush. I called my kiddos over to see the nest, cautioning them not to touch it, but encouraging them to take a closer look. Apparently I hadn't watered my roses in some time (no green thumb here, friends), because not only had the bird built her nest, but in it she had laid five beautiful speckled eggs.

This was a very exciting event for two pre-schoolers. Who am I trying to kid? I was pretty giddy myself! The science teacher in me started asking my children lots of questions about the birds; I was curious about what they already knew about our feathered friends. As a class-room teacher, I always begin science lessons by checking my students' prior knowledge; this helps me to see where they are in their current understanding of a topic and also to uncover any misconceptions they may have about the concepts. Drew (in three-year-old kindergarten that year) had been studying birds in school and already knew a lot about them: birds have feathers, eggs come out of their bodies, they build nests out of twigs and other things they find outside, and mommy birds feed their little ones worms and insects. When I asked the kids what the mommy bird does after she has laid the eggs, I got an interesting answer. Drew responded, "Well, the mommy bird goes on vacation and rests and then comes back to break the eggs open and let the baby birds out." Wow, the ideas that kids develop are so cool!

One of the hardest things about letting kids explore science on their own is resisting the urge to launch into an explanation of why their ideas are "wrong" and then explain everything. While this is definitely one way to

pass along knowledge about something new, I believe that it's not the most engaging way. So instead of "giving away the punch line," I decided to ask some more questions and then suggest an investigation. I told my kids, "You guys sure do have a lot of interesting ideas about birds, nests, and eggs! Let's think of a way we could study the bird that laid these eggs and learn more about it!" They were very excited and had some great ideas: "Could we bring the bird inside and let it live in our rooms?" "We can ask the bird some questions!" "We could look it up on Google." We weren't heading toward the observations I had in mind, so I tried to guide them with some scaffolding. I tried to summarize their ideas and then ask an open question to offer some direction: "Those are some great ideas. Since we can't take the bird inside or talk to the bird, how do you think we could learn about it? Are there other places where we could watch the bird?" Watching a lightbulb go on is so rewarding. Drew exclaimed, "We could watch the bird through the window and leave the nest right here on the patio!" And with that idea, we decided to watch (i.e., observe) the bird, the nest, and her eggs. The very first afternoon of observing the bird, the kids noticed that she left and returned to the nest multiple times. Drew looked at me with a big grin and said, "I guess she's not going on vacation like I thought!" Bingo! Now we had a genuine scientific exploration on our hands.

 ## How can we give children opportunities to explore science for themselves?

Give children an opportunity to explore before you explain

One of the most difficult aspects of teaching science in an inquiry-based approach is to teach in a different way than we were taught. Most of us grew up in a science class where we took notes on a topic, completed work sheets or confirmatory labs, and were subsequently tested on the material. Within the science curriculum I experienced as a student, there was little room for exploration. In other words, many of us simply didn't have a model for what it looks like to teach science using inquiry. As you are initially learning to implement inquiry in your own classroom, I advise you to start with a few basic ideas and then build from there. The first step in building a foundation for inquiry is to begin allowing your students to explore science before explaining it to them (Marshall and Smart 2013). In essence, you are giving them the opportunity to discover scientific ideas for themselves without "ruining the punch line." Think about how you feel if someone tells you the ending to a movie before you have a chance to watch it. Your motivation to see the movie likely decreases dramatically, as the mystery and intrigue are gone. Science is quite similar. Allowing students to explore an interesting and relevant scientific question or problem increases their motivation and actively engages them in the actual process of *doing* science.

There are multiple types of activities and learning experiences that provide an opportunity for students to explore a scientific concept. The first of these is the classic exploration of a scientific question by making a hypothesis and conducting an experiment. In many instances, young children may not be developmentally ready to complete an experiment individually. In this case, the teacher may choose to guide the students in posing a question, making a guess about what will occur, and then demonstrating the experiment for the group. The students still gain the benefit of a scientific exploration but at a level that is appropriate for their development. In one example from my kindergarten scientists, students made predictions about which object would sink or float in a tub of water. Students then took turns testing their predictions and learning about foundational concepts of density. The children were fascinated to see if their predictions were correct, and watched with anticipation as each object was lowered into the water. Through this exploration, the children began to notice that light plastic objects would float while heavy metal objects would sink. If I had simply told them which object would sink and float and then allowed them to place the objects in the water, the "hook" would have been missing, and the students would have lost their motivation to complete the activity.

Another common structure for an exploration is setting up stations or centers that allow students to engage with a scientific topic. For example, when my first-graders were studying animal classifications, I set up four centers for each type of animal that we would be studying: reptile, bird, mammal, and amphibian. Students took turns rotating through these stations and exploring objects such as photographs, real artifacts from each type of animal (e.g., feathers), iPads playing videos, and 3-D figurines. After each student had the opportunity to explore each station, we gathered as a class and created a list of the observations they had made about each type of animal. Students were able to actively describe characteristics of birds, reptiles, mammals, and amphibians because they had just had the opportunity to explore their features firsthand.

Explorations often stretch longer than a single day, as your students may need multiple days to observe a process. For example, if you want to engage your students in studying the process of sunlight's effect on plant growth, you will need to allow for a multiday exploration. In this scenario, students may develop a question to test on day 1 (e.g., Do plants need sunlight to live?), place their plants in sun/dark on day 2, and then observe these plants for several days to notice the long-term effects of sunlight on plant survival.

Allow students to explore meaningful questions

To engage children in meaningful inquiry, we need to provide opportunities for them to explore ideas and questions that are relevant and purposeful. We know that student motivation increases if students value a topic or concept (Wigfield 1994). In other words, we need to help our children answer the question, "So what?" When I was a graduate student, one of my professors routinely challenged us by asking, "So what?" when we would propose a new research idea. We had to be able to articulate the meaning or pragmatic value of each project or idea. We need to help our children answer the same "So what?" question about the science they are learning in our classes. By asking "So what?" we are really asking many questions, including, "Why does this matter in my life?" "Why does this matter in the world around me?" "Why is this important?" For example, I have always found the concept of severe weather to be the most popular with my students. Why? I believe it is because they all relate to this topic in a real and meaningful way. Most of us have personal experiences (often quite traumatic) with severe weather and its impact on our own lives. Most of my students engage with unrivaled interest when we broach the subject of tornadoes, hurricanes, and blizzards.

I've never witnessed quite the same exuberance, however, during a unit on electrical circuits. Why? Because students don't intuitively relate to wires, switches, and batteries—that is, until you put it into a context they *can* relate to, their homes. Noting the lack of fervor for this unit, I created an exploratory project for my fourth-graders in which they designed, built, and wired their dream home. When this topic was placed into a meaningful and relevant context, students quickly began to sketch, wire, and work to light up their model home. By the end of this unit, students were proud of their creations and could present an articulate description of open and closed circuits and other facets of electrical wiring. Finding a way for students to explore scientific concepts in a meaningful way is a critical first step in increasing student engagement and motivation in science.

Provide opportunities for "minds-on" learning

Activity mania is common in science. We often assume that just by allowing students to complete a fun science activity, they will magically absorb the science concepts the activity is intended to address. This couldn't be further from the truth. I observed a science lesson several months ago in which second-graders were completing an activity with the following setup: each student had a plate filled with milk and small drops of food coloring; each student then took a cotton swab dipped in dish detergent and stuck it in the middle of the plate of milk. Instantaneously, the plate of milk "exploded" with colors akin to tie-dye as the food coloring burst into rings inside the milk. The kids were amazed! The children were thrilled! But the children were *not* learning science. Now, the teacher *thought* she was doing a science activity. In fact, it was at best a fun filler between math and lunch.

Now, this may seem harsh, but allow me to explain. The milk, food coloring, and dish detergent activity would be fabulous if your students were studying polarity of molecules and surface tension in liquids. However, you won't find that in the second-grade science standards. Why? Because this science concept is not developmentally appropriate for seven-year-olds. There is no possible scenario in which the students would be able to develop a conceptual understanding of the science underlying the activity. If we include activities in our science instruction just because they are "fun" or "exciting," we aren't helping our students learn science. The activities we plan need to be closely related to the standards we are charged to teach at each grade level, and the fundamental science must be accessible to our students. Otherwise, the activities are hands-on but not minds-on.

When planning activities, we need to be able to clearly articulate the scientific idea we want our students to be able to experience. This is where guided inquiry differs from open inquiry. In an open inquiry situation, a teacher may present materials related to a topic and watch from a distance while children "do their own thing." In guided inquiry, the teacher is in the trenches with the children, constantly guiding them toward the primary scientific concepts of the activity and scaffolding the experience. The teacher always has the ultimate "destination" in mind in terms of learning objectives, and guides students along the path, steering them back on course if they stray too far from the topic. For example, I was teaching an inquiry-based lesson on states of matter in which my students were observing a glove filled with water, a frozen glove filled with ice, and a glove filled with air, like a balloon. The purpose of the lesson was for students to observe characteristics of solids, liquids, and gases and how they differ. As students were working in groups to examine each glove, I walked around asking questions to guide them such as, "What do you think would happen if you cut the glove open? What do you think is inside each glove?" Scaffolding this activity with guiding questions and monitoring the students constantly allowed them to focus on the important characteristics of each state of matter and progress toward the learning goals that I had developed for the lesson. Minds-on activities are the goal in inquiry-based instruction; activities lacking focus and direction will not result in meaningful learning for students in science.

CHAPTER FOUR
Physics in the Breezeway

How can we help children conduct a simple investigation?

When I was teaching first grade, our playground was located right beside a breezeway. It was a nice, covered area where many of my children chose to play with toys and escape the hot afternoon sun. There was one particular group of children who loved to race toy cars under the breezeway. They spent many days at recess creating their own grand prix on the smooth concrete beside the school and the adjacent sidewalk. One sunny afternoon, my students were racing a new red car that one of the boys had brought to school; it was one of those cars that you pull back and release, then watch it zoom speedily away.

As they played, I overheard the children talking about who could get the car to go the farthest. My ears perked up since they were teetering on the edge of an amazing physics exploration. Thankfully, first-graders still love their teachers and don't mind when they spontaneously join in their recess games, so my students welcomed me into their circle. I asked a question to get the kids thinking: "I wonder if this car would go faster if you pulled it back and let it go or if you just pushed it?" One little girl piped up, "I'm pretty sure pushing it hard will make it go the farthest." Her friend immediately objected with, "No. No. When you pull it back, it zooms superfast!" The students

began bickering among themselves, each convinced they were right and their friends were wrong. Eventually, they turned to me with wide eyes, expecting me to settle the argument. I grinned and suggested, "You know, we *could* test it."

The kids seemed delighted with this proposition (and also delighted to extend recess a bit), so we proceeded to set up a simple "test" to see how far the car would go given different conditions. To keep them invested in the process, it's important to let children take ownership of the activity as much as possible. If I had hijacked it and planned the experiment, we would have lost a valuable opportunity for my students to practice being the scientists. I asked them, "So, how do you think we could find out what makes the car roll farthest?" We went through a few ideas such as, "We could just search Google," and "We could roll them and see." With each suggestion, I tried to respect their ideas and point out the challenges of each suggestion (e.g., "We could search Google, but then we can't be sure they were using the same type of car as us.")

Collectively, we decided that rolling the car ourselves was the best idea, but we needed some structure for this investigation. Now, there are few, if any, six-year-olds who intuitively know how to set up a perfect scientific exploration, so this is where developmentally appropriate scaffolding comes in (Vygotsky 1978). I used targeted questions to "help" my students plan their investigation. For example, "Do you think the car should start at the same place each time?" "Do you think we should mark how far each car goes with chalk or something?" and "How could we roll the car a different way each time?" All the while, I built scientific vocabulary into the experience so that next time the words would be more familiar. For example, "OK, so you want to pull the car back and let it go the first time. This can be Trial 1." Ultimately, my students decided to do three trials: (1) pulling the car back and letting it go, (2) pushing the car without pulling it back, and (3) pulling the car back *and* pushing it. After each trial, the kids used chalk to mark where the car had stopped and walked from the beginning to the end to measure how many "paces" the car had gone. Since my students were learning about informal units of measurements in math, "paces" worked just fine and provided a great connection with our measurement unit. The concept of "distance traveled" was still intact.

We discovered that the car traveled farther when it we pulled it back *and* pushed it. We also talked a little about force and how objects move—beginner stuff but still allowing us to establish the foundation to later, more sophisticated physics concepts. Although it was time to go back to the classroom after we completed our investigation, my students now had even more questions they wanted to test. They spent the next few days at recess doing more explorations with the cars. I love it when science is cleverly disguised as play. One question they asked was: Does it matter if the car rolls on something "slanty" or "straight"? (i.e., "Does the incline of the ground make a difference in speed?" "Does it matter what the car is rolling on?" (e.g., grass, concrete, asphalt, etc.) One student noticed, "Hey! When the car hits a stick, it slows down!" Through this simple investigation, my first-graders had learned some basic concepts of motion that lay the foundation for more sophisticated ideas like velocity and speed in the years to come.

How can we help children conduct simple investigations?

Help children develop a good question that can be tested

All research begins with a question. Whether it is a scientist testing a potential treatment for cancer or a child testing the speed of a rolling car, a question is the starting point for any investigation. We need to help children develop questions that are accessible to them. In other words, can they carry out this investigation fairly independently? If we are the ones conducting the investigation for the child, they lose much of the value of being involved in the actual process of doing science. So the first hurdle of developing an effective investigation for young children is developing a question that can be explored fairly autonomously. As you noticed in the example above, scaffolding was still necessary to help my students plan and conduct their investigation. However, they were the ones actually carrying out the plan. Investigations should allow students to actively use their process skills (e.g., observation, measurement) on an appropriate developmental level.

Next, a scientific question needs to be measurable. In the example above, my students were not developmentally ready to use formal units of measurement (e.g., feet, meters), which tend to be too abstract for very young children. However, using informal measurements (paces) provided an effective way for them to measure the distance the car had traveled and to make comparisons between different trials. The use of informal measurements in science with young children provides a unit of measurement that they can relate to and comprehend. In another lesson with my first-graders, we used "paw lengths" to measure how tall our plants had grown; I printed off several cutouts of mouse paws, and we used those to measure how tall our plants had grown each day. Once students grasp the concepts of a "unit of measurement," the transition to using more formal units of measurement is seamless. It was no coincidence that the mouse-paw units I used with my class actually measured one inch in length; over time, students discovered that they could tape several mouse paws together to make their own mouse-paw ruler. Making the next small leap to using an actual ruler came naturally because they understood the concept. Just as we write learning objectives for our lessons that are measurable, the questions that students ask in science should also be measurable but in a way that is accessible to the child.

Encourage children to make a hypothesis about their question

By developing a hypothesis, or educated guess, about their question, children become more invested in the process. For young children, simply asking, "What do you think will happen?" provides students an opportunity to make a prediction about the upcoming experiment. Sometimes this is a new concept for students, and they can be a bit reluctant to make a guess when they are unsure about what is going to happen. As we prepare to test a question, I ask the class to help me come up with a list of things that could possibly happen. For example, if we are conducting an experiment on sinking and floating, the choices may be the following: The rock will sink, *or* the rock will float. I encourage students to write their hypotheses on pieces of paper and to place them in a basket for me to tally. In this case, I like to err on the side of keeping their hypotheses anonymous. Otherwise, in their minds young children may turn science into a contest of who is "right" and who is "wrong." Then I can quickly tally our guesses and record that X students have made a hypothesis that the rock will float, and X have made a hypothesis that the rock will sink. Students can still commit to a hypothesis, but this anonymous approach eliminates competition that could detract from the overall purpose of the activity.

As students gain more confidence in the scientific process of making a hypothesis, I like to provide more openness to this step, allowing each student to independently write a hypothesis in their journal instead of providing possible choices. This is an example of removing some of the scaffolds that we may originally put in place as students are learning a skill. Since the goal is to support children in developing autonomy in their learning, we have to remove scaffolds slowly as they begin to understand the process of developing and recording a hypothesis for an experiment. While students who are still struggling to develop a hypothesis on their own can then receive individual assistance, students who are ready to work more independently have the opportunity to do so.

Help children develop a simple, manageable plan to test their hypothesis

Developing an experiment can be a complex process that needs to be broken down into manageable parts. As mentioned in the example on page 17, I used multiple guiding questions to help my son consider the many choices made when designing an experiment. Working with a whole class, I have found that breaking this process down into several steps is helpful. After we have developed our question, we need to brainstorm ideas for how we could best test the question. I generally like to provide five to ten minutes of quiet time for students to individually think and sketch ideas for an experiment. Many children need time to process their thoughts instead of jumping immediately into a brainstorming session with the whole class in which students are yelling out a million ideas. Providing time for students to think at their own pace allows all students to access the question at hand and develop ideas of their own.

After this initial period of individual brainstorming, I then assign the students to small groups to share their ideas with their peers. I also find that at first children need explicit instructions about how to share their ideas in a group; we spend the first few weeks of school "practicing" how to take turns speaking and how to ask questions of group members if you don't understand what they have said. A lot of this initial group training borrows from the concept of "active listening" in which children listen to their peer and then summarize what the other person has said. I also like to give students a visual reminder of turn taking and provide each group with a token or object for this purpose. For example, I used plastic Easter eggs in one class, and whoever was holding the egg had permission to talk; I was trying to emphasize a rather corny idea that we were "hatching" good ideas, thus the egg. During this small-group time, students take turns sharing their ideas about possible experiments and then select one idea as the basis for the experiment their group will run. Keep in mind, I am always closely monitoring each group and initiating conversations to guide them toward an idea that will ultimately be successful in testing their hypothesis in an effective way. For a class with four to five groups, it is conceivable that we could have four to five very different experiments with the intent of testing one scientific question. I feel that it is beneficial for students to see that there is more than one way to test an idea, and it helps the class to ultimately value consideration of alternate ideas and diverse viewpoints.

After each experiment is designed, we make a list of all of the materials we will need, and students either write or draw a plan for conducting their experiment. I do my best to provide the materials each group requests, and children also ask parents to send in items that we may need. If an item is simply unavailable, we revise the experiment using a material that we can obtain. The next chapter details the process of supporting students in recording data and making sense of their findings once an experiment is "ready to roll."

CHAPTER FIVE
Now You See Me . . .

How can we ask children effective questions in science?

On a lazy Sunday afternoon by the pool, we had a few uninvited guests. You may be thinking about some distant third cousins stopping by for a surprise visit, but these were a different kind of uninvited guests, ones of the amphibian variety. See if you can spot them.

I suppose we were actually the ones crashing their party since this is technically *their* habitat. They were doing a good job at hiding out, perfectly camouflaging themselves against the rock around our pool. If you didn't see them the first time, here's a close-up.

Of course my kids weren't going to escape a "learning experience" on this particular Sunday afternoon—not when we were surrounded by cool, camouflaged creatures. I called over Drew and Claire and told them that some animals were playing "hide-and-seek" around our pool. Of course, they were instantly intrigued and started scouring the area for hidden animals. Drew asked, "Is it hiding under a rock?" Claire inquired, "Is it up in a tree?" I answered, "Nope. You're going to have to look pretty close to find these guys!" As they continued to search, I responded to their efforts with "getting warmer" or "getting colder" until they were practically staring the frogs in the beady little eyes. They slowly focused their eyes on our froggy friends, which blended in perfectly between white, speckled rocks.

Drew saw them first and shouted, "Wow! It's right here! It was right in front of us this whole time, and we didn't even see it!" We took a few minutes to let the excitement sink in and observe the frogs (there were four of them), and then I began to ask questions. First I asked, "So, why do you think we had a hard time finding these frogs?" Claire said, "Because they were between the rocks." I responded with, "Yes, they are between the rocks.

Do you have any other ideas about why we couldn't see them very well?" It's tricky to ask questions that will be beneficial for both Drew and Claire since they are a year apart in age and thus in their development. I like to ask questions that are simple enough to allow Claire to participate but open enough to give Drew the opportunity to follow up with more complexity. I redirected the question to Drew this time saying, "Claire made a great observation that the frogs were hiding in the rocks. Is there anything special about the rocks that would make it easier for the frogs to hide?" Drew studied the rocks and the frogs and then concluded, "Well, Mom, the frogs are the same color as the rocks!" Claire took a look again and joined in, "He's right! The rocks are white, and so are the frogs!"

I wanted to introduce an important vocabulary term, *camouflage*, and this was the perfect time to do it. While my kiddos had made sense of the concept of a frog blending in with the surrounding rocks, they had no explicit term for this, so this was an appropriate time to provide it. I told them, "You know, this frog is doing something really special. He is camouflaging himself against the rock! He's using his color to hide and blend in with things around him!" We didn't make a huge deal about the word, but I began to use it in our conversation about the frog. This enabled Drew and Claire to become familiar with the word and assimilate it into their schema about animals, but it didn't require any kind of formal definition.

There was one more concept relating to camouflage that I wanted to explore with the kids: purpose. I asked them, "So, why do you think the frog would need to hide?" Drew guessed first, "Because he's shy and doesn't want us to see him?" The kids are always assigning human characteristics to animals, probably based on the cartoons they watch with talking giraffes and singing crocodiles. I frequently have to point out that animals don't have the same feelings as humans and that usually the things they do have a purpose in helping them survive. I responded, "Well, Drew, that's a great guess. But remember that frogs aren't like us, they aren't shy or happy or sad. They usually do things to stay alive. So why would it help the frog stay alive to hide?" Claire suggested, "It might be hiding from Daddy because he might throw it in the woods!" (My husband, being a light sleeper, regularly complains that the frogs keep him awake at night and "relocates" them to the woods on the other side of our house whenever he gets the chance.) I told Claire, "Well, that's one reason they could be hiding! Is there anything else they could be hiding from?" Drew looked around and spied our yellow lab, Abby, sniffing around the edge of the pool. He exclaimed, "Abby! The frogs could be hiding from Abby! Or maybe other animals that are bigger and might eat them!" I smiled and nodded, "You're right, buddy. The frogs are camouflaged to protect them from predators that might eat them!" (Note the sly way you can introduce more science vocabulary; it's not a big deal, just making it part of the conversation.)

I told them that frogs aren't the only types of animals that can camouflage themselves; they were amazed and so intrigued by the idea of camouflage that they wanted to search the word on Google to see if we could find any pictures. Of course, we found thousands! As we perused the many, many images of animals that use camouflage to protect themselves, the kids would give simple explanations of why the camouflage would protect the animal. (For example, "The white fox is the same color as the snow!" "The bug looks just like a leaf!") In fact, they were so interested in camouflage in the animal world that I planned to develop an extension activity for us to do in the following days. Until then, we kept our eyes open for more animals playing hide-and-seek!

How do we ask children effective questions?

Ask open-ended questions

The first step in asking effective questions of young children is to consider the type of question you are asking. We are often prone to ask closed or yes/no questions of young children. (For example, Is the frog an amphibian? Does the car move faster on a smooth surface?) When we ask yes/no questions or questions requiring a simple one-word response, we limit our insight into what the students might be thinking (Chin 2007). The only way we can really understand how our children are comprehending the science at hand is to listen to them. And we often need good, open-ended questions to elicit this information from them. When teaching my undergraduates how to plan science lessons, I require them to explicitly list five to ten open-ended questions that they plan to ask their students during the lesson.

When planning for open-ended questions, the following stems are helpful to consider: What would happen if . . . ? Why do you think . . . ? What is the difference between X and Y? What do X and Y have in common? What do you know about X? You will notice that these questions are also written to encourage students to respond at a higher cognitive level. While questions requiring students to recall facts are certainly important, they cannot be the only questions we ask during science instruction. By encouraging students to explain, justify, compare, and contrast ideas, we are providing the support they need to think at a higher cognitive level. Asking follow-up questions to scaffold this process is also critical and is discussed next.

Ask follow-up questions

Traditionally, most classrooms operate using a questioning cycle that looks something like this: teacher asks a question, a student provides an answer, then teacher evaluates the student's answer (Smart and Marshall 2013). The problem with this type of questioning cycle is that it significantly limits the learning potential of the dialogue between teacher and students. When the sole purpose of asking questions is to evaluate a student's knowledge, we rarely get the opportunity to use questions as a springboard to go deeper with science concepts. Consider this alternate questioning scenario: teacher asks a question, student responds, teacher asks a follow-up question, student responds, teacher asks other students to comment on the student's response. Now we have dialogue. Now we have an actual conversation occurring in the classroom.

Asking follow-up questions is crucial to developing discourse in your science classroom. The following are examples of possible follow-up questions you can pose to your students: Can you tell me more? What made you think that? Why? Do you agree with his/her idea? These questions are the lifeblood of your classroom; they communicate to your students that their ideas are valid and important. Follow-up questions also provide the opportunity for students to communicate with their peers about science. One possible way to accomplish this is to ask students to follow-up on a response. For example, "John has an interesting theory about why the plant withered. What do you think about his idea? Can someone add to John's theory?" Follow-up questions can be a valuable tool in supporting students in thinking deeper about scientific concepts and using their peers' ideas as a springboard for new ideas.

Give wait time for students to respond

Young children often need additional time to process a question and respond. A general practice that I use with my students is to give five to ten seconds of wait time before calling on anyone. This allows students of all ability levels to hear the question, process the information, access their long-term memory, and formulate a response. It's actually quite astonishing how much brain activity goes into responding to a "simple" question! Behavior management strategies play into this aspect of questioning quite closely; it's difficult to use wait time if children are shouting out answers! I aim to create a classroom community of respect in which students have well-defined behavioral expectations and predictable consequences. If you expect students to raise their hands before providing an answer, it allows all students to have an equal opportunity to participate in classroom discourse, not just the "quickest" draw.

In a class of twenty students, it's not easy to keep track of the last time each child had on opportunity to answer a question; some days I can barely remember where I put my keys! I like to write each student's name on a Unifix Cube and keep them in a bucket so I can easily "draw" a name. I don't believe in using this in a punitive way, however; it's not intended to "catch" someone who is not paying attention or to raise anxiety in a child who struggles with shyness. When I call a child's name, they have the option of passing on that question or "calling a friend" to help them. When one child's name has been drawn, it's very easy to stack the Unifix Cubes on top of one another in the bucket to keep track of who has been called on and who has not. This way, I know I have at least provided an opportunity for each child to participate. It's also not unusual for us to use our "elbow partners" (i.e., the child right beside you) to whisper an answer to a question that I have posed to the class. Some children who are on the shier side feel comfortable sharing their answer one-on-one, and then that partner can say, "I like my partner's idea . . ." when we gather as a whole class to discuss.

Respond to incorrect answers without judgment

Incorrect answers are often a blessing in disguise. They don't have to be negative for the student. The manner in which we respond to a student's question can determine how that student will participate in the future and can affect their self-efficacy for science. The most important thing to remember about incorrect responses is that they provide you information; you can then use that data to guide your students toward the ultimate objectives for that lesson. For example, here are some positive responses to incorrect answers: "You're on the right track. Think about _____."; "I think you're thinking about _____. What do you remember about _____?"). Another way of addressing an incorrect answer is to redirect the question to another student but subtly. For example, if a student's answer is a tad off base, you could respond with, "You have some really good ideas. Could someone expand on what he/she is saying?" or "That's an interesting perspective. Could anyone add to this?" In this way, you acknowledge the student's efforts using a positive statement while also preserving their dignity and keeping the class discussion on track. Also, make sure to recognize the fact that some open-ended questions legitimately have more than one correct answer. Be careful not to shut down alternate solutions or perspectives just because they are different or unexpected. Allowing students to consider and analyze the ideas of their peers provides an opportunity for critical thinking and constructive criticism. Modeling these skills for your students can help your students evaluate ideas that differ from their own.

CHAPTER SIX
Timber!

How can we use visual representations and models to support student learning?

If a tree falls in the woods and no one is there to hear it, does it make a sound? If a pine tree falls outside your house in the middle of the night and crashes through the windshield of your car, does it make a sound? Yes. Yes, it does. In the South we rarely get snow. We get ice. Ice isn't pretty. You can't play in ice. You can't build an ice man. Ice causes trees to bend under its weight and eventually plummet to the ground. Or onto your car. (Yes, I'm speaking from personal experience.) So this story begins with a general assumption . . . when we have an ice storm in the South, trees will fall.

This winter, my children discovered this fact of life when a large pine tree fell across a road not far from our house. For some reason, it took nearly a week for the tree to be removed, so we had to take a long detour each day to bypass the blocked road. During this same ice storm, several tall pine trees fell in the woods behind our house, each making a startling crash but thankfully missing our home.

As my six-year-old son surveyed the fallen trees, I could see the wheels in his head begin to turn. He asked me, "Mom, why are these pine trees falling and none of the other trees seem to fall down?" I was delighted that he had made the observation that the pine trees were the most common victims in this ice storm. I asked him, "Well, why do you think that could be? Do you have any ideas?" He made several guesses related to the height and age

of trees: "Mom, maybe the pine trees are all just older and more frail, kind of like old people fall a lot." I tried to hide my smile but kept on with that line of questioning: "Well, son, these pine trees are actually younger than some of the older oak and maple trees in our yard. So they really aren't that old in comparison to the trees that are still standing." He began to look perplexed so I decided that we should make a model when we got inside to see if I could demonstrate why these pine trees were dropping like flies.

I hate to ruin the punch line, but the pine trees are more likely to fall because of their shallow root systems. They don't have an effective anchor when the ice starts building up. While we were able to observe the roots of the pine trees that had fallen, we couldn't make a comparison since the root systems of the other trees were still tucked away in the ground. When we went inside, I scoured the house to see what I could find to make a few root system models. I located some playdough to be our soil, straws for our trees,

and pipe cleaners for the roots. To represent a pine tree, I threaded the pipe cleaner through the straw and cut the "roots" off very short at the bottom. For the oak tree, I left a longer root system sticking out of the bottom of the straw.

I called Drew over to look at the two trees and to see if he could notice anything different about them. He quickly noticed that one had longer roots than the other. I asked some scaffolding questions like, "Why do you think a tree needs roots? What kind of roots did the pine tree have that we saw outside?" We then planned a simple experiment. We "planted" the trees in playdough and allowed them to dry overnight until the "soil" was firm. To focus Drew's thinking on the role of the roots in a tree's stability, I asked him, "Which tree do you think will be able to stand up longer if we push on the trunk? Do you think the roots will make a difference in how strong the tree is?" Drew made a guess that the tree with the longer roots might be stronger because "those roots will hang on tighter." Drew then took turns pushing on each tree; the pine tree model toppled right over, revealing its short root system. In comparison, the oak tree model was much harder to "topple," and it actually took some pulling and tugging on his part to uproot its longer root system. From this use of concrete models, I was able to teach my son something that could not be directly observed in our environment. We are routinely faced with science concepts that are difficult for children to conceptualize because they cannot be easily observed. Models are a valuable way to make these ideas attainable for our students and support their developing conceptual understandings about the world.

 ## How can we use visual representations and models to support student learning?

Ensure that visual representations are developmentally appropriate

Prior to a certain age, young children are going to struggle with understanding the idea that one item represents something else (Wigfield and Eccles 2002). In my experience, children around the ages of five and six are beginning to "get" the concept that one object can represent something else. For example, a kindergarten class I mentioned in a previous chapter had no problem understanding that a toothpick represented a bird's beak. However, when I taught a similar lesson to a kindergarten class of four-year-olds, many of the students struggled to make the connection that the toothpick was supposed to be a bird's beak. These younger students viewed the toothpick as just that—a toothpick. In that instance, it would have been more appropriate to use an actual picture of a bird's beak for children who were not quite ready to make this abstract leap in their minds. When working with children five and older, simple models in which an object is intended to represent something else will be effective. In children younger than five, visual representations can still be used, but they need to be much more explicit. For example, when teaching a lesson on the parts of a plant, I would use either real or silk flowers instead of pipe cleaners and construction paper to represent the stem and leaves. While those materials may yield beautiful art projects (and there is always a place for arts integration in science), very young children are simply not developmentally ready to understand a complex representation, and the actual science will be lost.

Develop a collection of "odds and ends"

As a classroom teacher, I always kept a bin of random objects and, for lack of a better word, junk. Over time I accumulated screws, pieces of string, springs, parts of old toys, and a hundred other items that seemed destined for the trash can. But when I needed a model of some abstract scientific concept, I was often able to produce something very useful from all that junk. Now, in a perfect world I would have planned ahead for these specific models and had everything prepared, and I would have anticipated every question a student could ever ask . . . but we don't live in a perfect world. So sometimes you have to be prepared to ad lib.

I'm reminded of a lesson that I was teaching on solids, liquids, and gases. I hadn't planned to address the molecular structure of these states of matter (this was third grade for goodness sake!), but one of my clever students asked, "Mrs. Smart, what makes ice and water different. I mean, what *really* makes them different?" A few weeks prior to that lesson, I had been given a bag of marbles, which promptly went into my bin of random things. I went over and grabbed the marbles and gave one to each of my students. I explained that the marbles were going to be the separate parts of water, better known as molecules. First, I had them take all of their marbles and put them in the center of the room so that they were all touching each other. This, I explained, is what happens inside a solid; the molecules are extremely close together. Then I had the students spread out the marbles on the floor so they were at least a foot apart and no longer touching. This, I explained, is how a liquid looks inside. Finally, I instructed the students to take their marbles and put them at the far edges of the room, adding as much distance between them as possible. I explained that the molecules of a gas act like this. When you have to think quick and come up with a physical representation off the top of your head, it helps to have a junk box full of possibilities!

Use models to bridge the gap between the abstract and the concrete

I think of models as a scaffold for students as they grapple with abstract ideas. These abstract concepts may be out of reach initially, but with a concrete representation as support, students can reach an understanding (Kolloffel, Eysink, and de Jong 2011). A major philosophy that grounds my science instruction is the concept of moving students from concrete to abstract (this actually guides my mathematics instruction as well, but I'll save that idea for another book.) It's like looking at a map. We live in a world of the concrete, so that's where we begin; our destination is a conceptual understanding of abstract ideas that we don't observe in daily life. Think about a child who is trying to understand the seasons. Talk about an abstract idea! The world you are standing on is whirling around a big ball of fire, and this world's imaginary path around the ball of fire gives you summer and winter? No, that's not something most kids can relate to at first. So we have to move them toward it gradually, beginning with the concrete and introducing progressively more abstract representations. For example, we begin to tackle the concept of seasons with a very concrete model, usually involving a lamp and an actual globe. When students act out the journey of the earth around the sun, they can touch, feel, and experience the concept. This is usually the part of a lesson where we may be tempted to move directly to a work sheet that employs a more complex visual representation of the scientific concept (e.g., a 2-D model of the earth, sun, and elliptical orbits). Not so fast. Moving directly from a playacting scenario to a visual diagram is asking students to make a huge leap in their thinking, and you are bound to lose a few students. A logical next step is to make the model slightly more abstract, perhaps by using large cutout photographs of the earth and sun to plot an orbit on a big space poster in order to gradually convey how the idea transfers to 2-D. After students can successfully explain the concept using a community 2-D model, it is conceivable that they would be able to understand a work sheet with a more advanced representation of the earth's revolution around the sun. The move from concrete to abstract must be scaffolded and monitored to ensure that students are making the necessary translations between concept and representation. With very young children, this progression may be much simpler: actual apple, photograph of an apple, drawing of an apple. Never assume that a child will automatically make the sophisticated jump from concrete to abstract without your bridging the gap along the way.

CHAPTER SEVEN
Stayin' Alive

How do we adjust science instruction based on student learning?

When I was teaching third grade, we took a field trip to the zoo. While we were there, we went to a special program that introduced several animals that utilized mimicry and camouflage to survive in their environment. My students were particularly intrigued by the chameleon and how it could change colors to blend in with its surroundings. When we returned to our classroom, I decided to develop an extension activity to explore the concept of camouflage in a different context. This activity was originally planned to take place outdoors. You'll quickly realize from the pictures below that this did not happen as planned. It rained on the day I had planned this activity, so we moved everything indoors. As my college choral director instilled in me, "Adjust, adapt, and accept." And so we did.

All of the critters in the picture to the right are the starting point for this activity. I gathered my students around the science table in our room and showed them the animals I had laid out. I wanted to make the activity as open as possible, so I told them, "Choose an

animal, and find a place in our classroom for it to hide. I'm going to pretend to be a lion that is hunting for your animal. The only rule is you can't hide your animal under anything or inside of anything." I was trying to emphasize the concept of camouflage and an animal's ability to blend in with its environment, so I didn't want this activity to rapidly descend into a simple game of hide-and-seek. After my students had a few minutes to hide their animals, I went "hunting." It wasn't hard to find the first animal; Josie had placed her green lizard on a white box.

This was a great way for me to realize that Josie didn't "get" the concept of camouflage yet. A green lizard on a white box is definitely an easy meal for a predator. I pretended to quickly "eat" the lizard and then asked Josie, "Do you think the lizard was able to hide from the lion very well? Why do you think I found him so quickly?" She replied, "Mrs. Smart, you are a good hunter!" While I was flattered that Josie was impressed by my hunting prowess, we needed some scaffolding to help focus on the concept at hand. I asked Josie to think back to the chameleon we saw at the zoo. "Josie, why was the chameleon able to hide in the leaves at the zoo?" She thought a moment and then said, "It was the same color as the leaves." I replied, "Aha! So tell me about the lizard you just tried to hide. Is he the same color as the box?" I watched a little lightbulb go off, and she said, "No! He's green, and the box is white, so you could see him really good." I encouraged her to try to find a better place for him to hide and then I would go hunting for him again. Here is the next spot she chose for her lizard:

Bingo! Now we're getting somewhere. This time as I went "hunting" for the lizard, I pretended that I couldn't find him and the "lion" went home hungry. Josie took great delight in "showing" me where the lizard was hiding and said, "He hid on the green truck, and he is green so you couldn't find him this time! He was camouflaged!" Now, I know what you're thinking; a toy garbage truck isn't exactly a naturally occurring habitat. Keep in mind I had intended to do this activity outside, but the rain kept us indoors. We're working on the *concept* of camouflage and the *purpose* of this adaptation for survival, so the context is not our primary focus. I noticed several other students had overheard my conversation with Josie and consequently went scampering across the room to move their animal to a new hiding place. It was clear to me that most of my students still didn't have a full understanding of the concept of animal camouflage.

I had originally planned for this to be our only extension activity, but I needed to make some adjustments to my instruction since we still needed additional practice on this concept. I decided to turn the tables on this activity and allow the students to be the hunters this time. It was my hope that actually hunting for hidden animals would help them see which were easiest to find and which were more difficult to locate. I took the creatures and hid them in our classroom. I intentionally "camouflaged" about half of the critters and left the other half out in the open, hoping to emphasize the differences as students hunted.

My little predators rushed in and quickly "devoured" the animals that were easy to spot. I told them to "freeze" for a moment and think about why they had found those animals so quickly. One student responded, "Well, we found them quick because giraffes are yellow and whales are grey and they were on the red rug." I responded with, "Great! So were those animals camouflaged?" A chorus of "Nos" chimed in, and one student inquired, "So did you camouflage any?" I told them to unfreeze and keep hunting. The "predators" eventually found the rest of the animals but not nearly as quickly as the first ones. In fact, I had hidden a blue squid on a blue plate beside my desk, and the students missed that one altogether. After the "hunt," one student asked a great question: "We found the prey even though some of them were camouflaged. I thought it made them invisible to the predators?" This was a great point and a common misconception; many young children believe that camouflage is akin to an "animal superpower" that gives them a magical invisibility, completely protecting them from their predators. I answered him with the following questions, "Were the chameleons at the zoo invisible? Could a predator *eventually* find an animal that was camouflaged?" He answered me, "No, the chameleon wasn't invisible, it was just harder for us to see him. We saw him eventually." And that's the key: *harder* to find them but not *impossible*. Thanks to some adjusting of this lesson based on real-time data on student understanding, my class was demonstrating a conceptual understanding of animal camouflage and its benefits for animal survival.

How do we adjust instruction based on student learning?

Constantly "check the pulse" of your class

How would you feel if you went in for major surgery and the anesthesiologist checked your vitals before surgery and then again at the end? Would that seem sufficient to you? Hopefully not, if you are looking to make it out of the surgery alive! A lot can happen during a procedure, which requires the anesthesiologist to constantly monitor a patient's blood pressure, pulse rate, and other critical vitals. This continuous monitoring results in adjustments to the medication and oxygen during surgery to react to this patient data. It isn't acceptable to simply wait until the end of the operation to see if the patient is still alive. So why would we treat our classrooms any differently?

So often we wait until the end of our instruction to see if our students are still with us. In many classrooms, the teacher doesn't realize that students are failing to meet the learning objectives until the end of a lesson or unit, at which point it is sometimes too late to make any meaningful changes. As teachers, we need to monitor our students continuously to assess their understanding in "real time." This process of constantly monitoring student understanding and adjusting instruction accordingly is known as formative assessment (Black et al. 2004). We can accomplish this through a variety of informal methods such as conversations with students, whole group check-ins such as "thumbs up/thumbs down," and observing closely as students communicate and work. More formal methods of continuous monitoring include checklists, science journals, student products (e.g., drawings), and quick-check quizzes. All of this data can inform us about the current state of students' learning; the next, critical step is using this information to make adjustments to our instruction in response to our students' level of understanding.

Give yourself permission to deviate from your original plan

We often regard our lesson plans as documents etched in stone. However, if we are going to be open to letting our students' learning guide our instruction, we have to be willing to adjust these plans as necessary. This is the essence of formative assessment, using student data to make adaptations to our instruction. This is not an easy process. I consider this one of the most challenging aspects of teaching. We spend so much time planning every lesson and learning experience that going "off the map" can be intimidating and uncomfortable. However, if we really want our instruction to result in meaningful learning, we have to be willing to revise our plan if needed.

For example, I was teaching a lesson on rock formations to my third-graders and was cruising along, feeling great about how it was going. We had a series of hands-on activities to demonstrate the various types of rock formations and their characteristics. When I gave the unit test, I fully expected my students to ace it, but the class average was a fifty-two. My class was collectively failing the objectives for our earth science unit, and I was shocked! The worst part was that I was out of time on this unit; we were supposed to be finished with rocks and moving on to life science the next week. But I knew I couldn't move on in good conscience, knowing my class was completely missing a very critical science concept. So I spent the weekend revising the lesson plans for the following week, figuring out how to reteach the concepts with which my students were struggling. It was then that I realized that I had not been very good at monitoring my students' learning in the weeks we had been studying earth science. If I were an anesthesiologist, my patients would have never made it out of surgery. This was a turning point for me as an educator, and I became committed to constant, frequent monitoring of my students' learning *before* it was too late to make adjustments. This experience forever changed the way I teach science, and consequently the way my students learn.

Assess prior knowledge to uncover science misconceptions

Assessing students' prior knowledge can be both eye-opening and highly entertaining. The notions that preschool and elementary-age children have about science never fail to amaze me. I once taught a little boy who was convinced that rain was formed by tears of angels. This was such an innocent and sweet misconception, but the boy was quite resistant to changing his thinking. As we continued to study weather, I was surprised by how stable this misconception was despite many activities and discussions that presented evidence to the contrary. Uncovering these science conceptions at the beginning of a lesson is critical to understanding each child's starting point and the ideas that will ultimately influence learning (Songer and Gotwals 2012). In this case, the idea that rain is formed from angel tears was an explanation passed on by the child's grandmother; ideas learned from revered family members are quite challenging to address and can often result in a cognitive dissonance for young children.

Children can also develop misconceptions based on ideas that they see on television and in movies. One common misconception I have seen in young children is the idea that animals have human characteristics, such as the ability to speak an actual language. Many cartoons and movies feature animals that act similarly to humans, so children come to accept this as a form of reality. Uncovering these misconceptions early can provide the teacher with much-needed information about how to begin chipping away at these inaccurate ideas. There are several effective ways to challenge misconceptions without flat out shooting them down. One of the most common ways is to present a discrepant event. For example, if a child has the misconception that all metal sinks in water, you could perform a demonstration that shows how a metal paperclip can float.

Another strategy for addressing misconceptions is to allow the child to struggle with some cognitive dissonance. Cognitive dissonance arises when a personal belief or idea meets conflicting information (Ormrod 2006). For example, my son recently developed a fear of spiders. This fear came about in an unfortunate way—I was watching the movie *Arachnophobia*, thinking that my son was playing upstairs in his room. Without me knowing it, he had snuck downstairs and was standing behind me in the doorway watching in secret. (Don't judge—this kid is practically a ninja in his ability to sneak up without me noticing.) He happened to walk in during the scene in which the large spider jumps out of a bush and attacks a man. Drew was quite traumatized by this, and we spent a lot of time talking about how this was just a movie, that (1) large hairy spiders are not indigenous to our state, and that (2) spiders don't just attack unprovoked. But even with all of these well-crafted explanations, Drew's misconception that spiders were mean, human-hunting beasts persisted. Then I remembered that Drew had held a hairy tarantula at a birthday party not long before. One of his friends had a party in which the "Critter Keeper" brought many animals to show the children. I found the picture of Drew holding the tarantula and showed it to him. I asked him, "Drew, if all spiders are just waiting to attack people, why didn't this spider try to attack you?" I could see the wheels turning in his head, and I knew that I had managed to create some cognitive dissonance in his mind. He was struggling between the misconception that all spiders were evil and the counterexample of Rosie, the tame tarantula. I can't say that we completely overcame the spider fear that day, but we did make strides toward breaking down that misconception. Creating cognitive dissonance opens the door for children to see that their misconceptions may be faulty, allowing them to begin to think about revising their thoughts.

One word to the wise—misconceptions can be very stable in young children. In other words, it can be difficult to get them to change their minds. In regard to the angel-tears misconception, for example, the little boy had learned this from his grandmother, whom he deeply loved and respected. It's not easy to go up against grandma! Sometimes the best you can do is present an alternate viewpoint and plant that seed of conceptual understanding to bloom in a future science classroom.

CHAPTER EIGHT
Making a List, Checking It Twice

How can we support children in representing data in developmentally appropriate ways?

You may remember that in the introduction to this book I talked about the question my children posed one morning at breakfast: How long does it take a seed to grow into a plant? This question could have easily been answered by consulting Google, but we chose to take the road less traveled and investigate the question ourselves. We went to the store that afternoon, and my children picked out some cute little animal pots.

We used the potting soil and grass seed we already had at the house to start an experiment. The kids planted their grass seeds, watered them, and then found a sunny place to let them grow. I told them that we were going to observe our plants every day and try to answer the question, "How long does it take a seed to grow into a plant?" We made some guesses (hypotheses) about how long it would take until we could see the grass seeds beginning to sprout. When the kids were younger, we defined "a day" as how many times we would have to wake up before something happens. For example, if we were going to the zoo in four days, I would tell them, "We have four wake-ups until we go to the zoo!" It's especially helpful for Claire, age three, to think about a day as something very concrete, such as the number of "wake-ups" before an event. Drew is beginning to think more abstractly about elapsed time, so he is developing an understanding that a day is a cycle that has a distinct beginning and end. So, Drew guessed that the plant would sprout in two days, while Claire guessed that it would take "five wake-ups" until the grass would sprout, or become visible above the soil.

When we first began exploring this question, I wanted to provide a simple, developmentally appropriate way for my kiddos to collect data on the length of time it took their grass seeds to sprout. This is where things get a little abstract . . . and abstract thinking isn't easy for most three- and four-year-olds. The idea that a chart or picture could represent something else, such as plants growing, is not intuitive. Children at this age think very concretely; however, they are completely capable of collecting simple data and recording their findings if the experience is scaffolded. I developed a chart that would allow the kids to observe their plant every day and answer the simple question: "Do we see grass yet?" This is a very concrete, observable question that requires a straightforward answer: yes or no. We talked about how it would feel to see grass growing; Drew and Claire both agreed that it would make them feel happy, so we paired a smiley face (☺) with a check mark (√), and that became our symbol for "yes." This is an effective way to connect their prior experience with the familiar (☺ and ☹) symbols to assign meaning to more abstract symbols, √ or an X. We used the same process to identify a sad face (☹) with an X, signifying "No, we didn't see any grass today." I also chose to use colors to help the kids differentiate between each outcome (yes or no) and also to expose them to the idea of color coding data. Here's the original data sheet:

We observed our plants daily and marked either a √ or an X based on what we observed. This was also a great exercise in recognizing numerals for each day and gave us a chance to work on fine-motor skills! Here's a shot of us in action—little scientists busy recording data.

Finally, on day 3, the grass sprouted! Now, wasn't that more fun than looking up the answer on Google? Here's a photo taken several days later, when the grass clearly needed a haircut.

 ## How can we support children in representing data in developmentally appropriate ways?

Record meaningful data

Children are more motivated to engage with scientific concepts, even representing data, when the topic is meaningful to them. Since learning to graph and chart information is a science process skill, it often needs to be practiced in a context apart from actual science content. In my classroom, we graphed data that was interesting and relevant to my students. For example, we often made simple graphs about favorite foods, the preferred classroom pet, favorite movies, and the colors everyone was wearing on a particular day. These are topics that are relevant and concrete and provide an excellent context to practice representing data in a graphic way. When it came time to transfer these graphing skills to science, it was not a new or novel concept. My students also loved to develop tally charts; one of our favorites was to track the number of compliments the class collected from the related arts teacher, the principal, and so on. The class would receive extra recess when they reached fifteen compliments, so this graph was especially motivating to them. Encouraging students to graph meaningful data increases their value and efficacy for this process skill and prepares them to use these skills in the context of science data collection.

Model various methods of representing data in the classroom

I believe in the power of modeling for learning (Bandura 1989). As a teacher, I always wanted my students to see me graphing and representing class data so that they would see that the practice has purpose. I routinely graphed a variety of things: attendance, number of books read by the class, class averages on spelling tests, and weather-related data. I designated a specific bulletin board in the classroom as our "Data Center" and made sure that I was consistent in updating our graphs. By modeling the importance of graphing and representing data on a class level, I conveyed to my students that I valued the practice. I tried to vary the types of graphs that I kept for the class, rotating between tally charts, bar graphs, line graphs, and pictographs. I also incorporated simple checklists into our daily routine as we marked our completion of the activities of the day. By modeling the representation of data, we developed a classroom culture in which this was normative. I often observed my students copying these charts into their own notebooks "just for fun." I also encouraged parents to model graphing and representing data at home and provided them with ideas for how they could accomplish this. Many of the parents began to graph routines such as bedtime and "screen time" and used checklists for chores and household responsibilities. Modeling is a powerful practice and can be accomplished by simply allowing your students to observe you engaging in the process of data gathering.

Develop simple templates that you use often

When students are learning a new skill, simplicity is usually the best approach. I developed simple graphic and charting templates that could be applied to a variety of circumstances. Throughout the year, I would slowly introduce each template, and then we would spend several weeks learning to use it in different contexts. By midyear, even my first-graders had developed a small stable of graphing tools to use as we studied science. In addition to representing numerical (quantitative) data, I also like to provide graphic tools for my students to represent descriptive (qualitative) data. When students develop skills for effectively organizing information, numeric or descriptive, it helps them to process and later retrieve this information more effectively (Georghiades 2004). For example, I routinely used Venn diagrams, bubble maps, and flow charts with young children. Even if they are not developmentally ready to create their own charts, being able to see the information in an organized manner can help students encode these ideas more efficiently in their long-term memory. With my older children, we routinely took notes in graphic organizers to model good study habits in science and in other content areas.

Give your students an opportunity to talk about their data

When students are learning to graphically depict their data, it is critical to give them opportunities to "talk through" their graphs and assign meaning to their data. This can be accomplished in several ways. The most traditional route is allowing students to give small class presentations about their data, which is certainly an acceptable practice. However, time constraints can limit the ability to do this regularly, and science is generally the subject allotted the least amount of time in the curriculum (National Research Council 2012). Another method to accomplish this goal is through peer conversations. Students can turn to their "elbow partner" or the students in closest proximity and give an elevator talk about their data. What is an elevator talk, you might ask? Imagine you step onto an elevator with someone and you're tasked with the challenge of explaining your data in the time it takes for you to ride up to the next floor. Generally, an elevator talk is a thirty-second explanation of a topic that is well suited to a brief synopsis in graph form.

(For example, the flowers in the sunshine lived longer than the flowers in the dark.) This type of elevator talk is also easy to adjust if you want to include more information; you can simply say you are traveling to the fifth floor, tenth floor, and so on. It's also a great way to slip in some mathematics! I also like to encourage my students to communicate their data to their parents. I would often send home a sheet of paper, asking parents to record word for word what their student told them about their graph or chart. This is a powerful way to communicate with parents about the skills you are working on in school, and it also provides a formative assessment to gauge students' understanding of a scientific concept (Yin, Tomita, and Shavelson 2014).

CHAPTER NINE
Baby Bird Birthday

How can we encourage children to communicate their scientific ideas in multiple ways?

You may remember that in chapter 3 we were waiting expectantly for some new arrivals at our home. My children and I had discovered a bird nest in one of the rose bushes on our patio. As a science exploration, my children had been observing the nest each day, noticing how often "Momma Wren" visited the nest and making predictions about when the birds would hatch.

We were eating breakfast on our porch one morning when the kids saw Momma Wren fly out of her nest, so they rushed over to take a look at the eggs in the nest. It's amazing how comfortable Momma Wren has gotten with us; often she will just watch us when we're playing right around her nest. We did have a scare last week when we thought our dog, Abby, had eaten our "science project," but it turned out to be a *different* bird. (Our apologies if our dog ate someone else's science project.) But I digress. So when the kids went over to see the eggs, they told us, "The daddy bird is in the nest too." I explained to them that the daddy bird isn't involved at this point, which my husband was a little offended to discover. But the kids kept insisting there was another bird in the nest. Sure enough, there in the nest were several wiggling, tiny baby birds.

Drew exclaimed, "I see a beak!" Claire said, "They look like ducks!" (Not really sure where she came up with that one, but we went with it.) When the bird first laid her eggs a couple weeks ago, I discovered that my kids had a misconception about how the birds got out of the eggs. Drew thought the momma bird sat on the eggs to break them open so the baby birds could get out. This was a great opportunity to revisit that idea. I asked Drew, "So, it looks like the baby birds are out of their eggs. Do you think there was any way for them to get out without the mommy bird's help?" Without explicitly answering the question for him, I was hoping to latch on to his initial observation that the baby bird has a beak. He looked at the baby birds again, then looked at me with a smile and said, "Mommy! What if the baby bird used its beak like a hammer and broke its way out of the shell all by itself!" It's so awesome to see these lightbulb moments. I followed up by asking Drew to show me what he meant. He looked a little confused, so I said, "OK, pretend you are a baby bird, and you have a shell around you. How would you use your beak to get out?" Both of my kids love "playacting" right now, so Drew and Claire both pretended to use their "beaks" to break out of their imaginary shells. Dramatic play is a great way to help young children communicate their ideas in science; it allows them to experience ideas that are rather abstract in a more concrete way.

I wanted to "ride the wave" of their excitement about the baby birds hatching, so we went inside and read a great nonfiction book we had checked out from the library to learn some things about birds that we weren't able to observe directly, like how the bird forms inside the egg and how the bird makes her nest. I wanted to find a way for my kids to communicate the ideas they had learned about nests, birds, and eggs. Communicating ideas is a major theme in science, but obviously three- and four-year-olds aren't quite ready to make a PowerPoint presentation or write

a paper. The Reggio Emilia Approach to early childhood holds a belief about the "hundred languages of children," which is the idea that young children have many ways to communicate other than written words or spoken words (Malaguzzi 1993). They can communicate using various forms of art, drama, music, dance, and so on. I decided that I would give my kids the opportunity to communicate their new knowledge of birds through painting. It's important to let children represent their ideas without trying to make them fit our ideas of how to "correctly" represent a bird or eggs or a nest.

Claire's painting on the previous page is very abstract but also very developmentally appropriate. When she described her painting to me, she said, "The purple is the nest, the babies are orange, the momma bird is brown, and the rest is the plant and the porch." In her perfect, three-year-old way, she was able to communicate her ideas about the birds we have been observing. Learning to communicate ideas about science doesn't have to be complicated, but in any form, it's fascinating.

 ## How can we encourage children to communicate their scientific ideas?

Encourage children to verbalize their ideas about science

Giving children opportunities to talk about science is critical for multiple reasons. One of these reasons is that verbalizing scientific ideas is the essence of what it means to be a scientist. Communicating is a process skill that lays the foundation of a child's ability to relate ideas about the world around them (Smart and Marshall 2013). As teachers, we are the gatekeepers to the right to communicate in our classrooms. We set and monitor procedures for participation, such as raising hands to speak, taking turns, and talking to their peers at appropriate times (van Zee et al. 2001). When I was a graduate student, I spent many hours in science classrooms conducting research on inquiry-based instruction and the many features of student-centered instruction. One of the most notable features of these classrooms was the way in which students communicated with the teacher and with their peers. Many of the teachers I observed consistently provided students with opportunities to share their ideas with the whole class, in small groups, and with partners. I was struck by the amount of talking that went on in these classrooms! But instead of being distractive, the talk was focused on science and added to the student learning that was taking place.

Our own philosophies about classroom management can either facilitate or hinder the opportunities for students to communicate their ideas in science. In classrooms where the teacher maintains tight control, procedures tend to be rigid, and students often have limited opportunities to engage in conversation with their peers or to offer their ideas during instruction. While no one would argue the importance of an orderly classroom—you can't teach in chaos—we all need to examine the effects of our management system. When I was a first-year teacher, I assumed that a noisy classroom was "wrong." I tended to shy away from situations that would result in a loud classroom, often opting for individual work or tightly controlled activities with minimal peer interaction. Thankfully, a mentor said something to me that challenged this idea.

I was teaching a science lesson when my mentor came to observe me. It was so quiet in the classroom you could hear a pin drop. Granted, the lesson went off without a clear hitch, and I was feeling pretty good about how I had kept my class focused and on task. As we sat down to debrief about the lesson, my mentor looked at me with a warm smirk and said, "You know . . . learning is loud." Really? She was asking me to allow my children to be loud? This flew in the face of most teaching that I had seen modeled during my teacher education program. It also gave me a sigh of relief; she was giving me permission to loosen the reins a bit—permission to allow my students to be children and to embrace everything that came along with that, including a little rise in the volume level. As I allowed my students more opportunities to talk to each other and to me, I began to finally "hear" them. I realized how important it is to truly give children a voice, to allow them opportunities to verbalize their ideas. This is also tantamount to formative assessment; it is nearly impossible to adjust instruction based on student learning if you have no idea what's going on inside their heads. The only way to find out is to encourage them to speak up and to provide ample opportunities for this to occur.

Provide multiple methods for children to communicate about science

A few years ago, I had the opportunity to spend several weeks in Reggio Emilia, Italy, home of one of the most famous early childhood educational approaches in the world. In Reggio, teachers talk frequently about the hundred languages of children (Edwards, Gandini, and Forman 1993). The idea is that children have many valuable ways to communicate their ideas, many of which we never recognize. While in Reggio, I had the rare opportunity to visit several official Reggio preschools, which are usually closed to outside visitors. In one Reggio preschool, I visited a classroom of five-year-old children who were just returning from an outside playtime. The class had been cooped up inside all morning due to the rain, so when the sun finally peeked out later in the day, the teachers took the opportunity to shuttle the children outside to burn off some energy. While they were playing in this post-rain period, the children spotted a rainbow in the sky. They had all become fascinated with the rainbow and had asked their teachers many curious questions about it. The Reggio approach believes in listening to the questions that children ask and letting their natural curiosity guide the curriculum. As the children filed back in from playtime, the teachers began taking out paints, clay, and colorful tissue paper and encouraged the children to represent the rainbow with a variety of engaging materials. As photography is not allowed inside the Reggio schools, I can only tell you that I was so inspired by the way in which the children scrambled to capture the beauty of the rainbow in different mediums. In another part of the room, a teacher turned on the light table (a table with a Plexiglas cover that's lit from within) for children to experiment with how light shines through materials of various textures and thickness. In another section of the room, the teacher produced an overhead and prisms so children could recreate the rainbow on a screen in the room. In these Reggio preschools, students are routinely provided with multiple ways of communicating their ideas about science. This is the embodiment of the appreciation of the hundred languages of children that is engrained in this Italian culture and the way in which they value a child's ideas.

Develop a classroom culture that values students' ideas

A key aspect of encouraging students to communicate their ideas in science is developing a classroom culture that values these ideas. One way to begin building this culture is to find small ways to give students ownership of their classroom. This idea is also demonstrated in the Reggio classrooms, in which student work and student-made products are in sight in every corner of the school.

A common characteristic of Reggio schools is providing children with a sense of ownership of their work. In a visit to a Reggio preschool, I observed that the children had been busy planting a vegetable garden, and their art-work marked each type of plant in the garden. While an adult could have easily made markers for the vegetables, students were encouraged to take ownership of every step in the process of planting and caring for their garden. When we allow our students to express their ideas in the small details, we send the message that their ideas are valued and significant.

Another way that we can create a classroom culture in which student ideas are valued is to document our collective journey in science exploration. In this era of ever-present smartphone cameras and digital recording devices, consistently documenting the work going on in your classroom is more convenient than ever. An effective method for keeping a record of students' learning in science is by creating documentation panels (Rinaldi 1998). These panels, usually displayed at the entrance to the classroom, use pictures and students' journal entries to document recent activities and learning that has been taking place in science. These panels serve as a communication tool between the class and visitors and provide a starting point for students to explain to classroom visitors what they have been learning in science. In addition, these documentation panels serve as a communication tool between teachers and parents, as they can be scanned and placed on a class website. Students can actively contribute to these documentation panels using their sketches, photographs, journal entries, and other visual representations to further communicate their scientific ideas.

CHAPTER TEN
Shake, Rattle, and Roll

How can we make science relevant to the lives of young children?

In our city, we are so lucky to have a fabulous children's museum. On any given Saturday, hundreds of children explore and play in the many interactive exhibits. The children's museum is a popular field trip destination, so I have escorted many groups of children through the three floors of educational fun. There are many exhibits that relate both directly and indirectly to our science standards, but my very favorite is the earthquake table. Few topics captivate a child's interest like the prospect of demolition. Kids are naturally drawn to the excitement and drama of building something and then sending it tumbling to the ground. The earthquake table provides the perfect setting to connect science to a real-world concept and emphasize problem-solving skills, both of which play an important role in the Next Generation Science Standards (Achieve 2013).

Knowing that the earthquake table is an exhibit I want to highlight during any trip to the children's museum, I do a little prep in the classroom before we go. I first show the class pictures of various types of buildings and have them predict which ones would be more likely to withstand an earthquake. We talk about the Richter scale and also watch a few video clips of actual earthquake damage so they can understand the magnitude of destruction that can result from this geological phenomenon. Invariably, I know I will not be able to work with each student during the field trip, since they will be moving through the exhibits in groups, so I preview the earthquake task for them. The main objective for this task is for the student to design a structure that could withstand a fairly strong earthquake, providing an excellent real-world tie-in as well as an opportunity for problem solving. Each student sketches a design they want to try to construct during the field trip, proposing an initial solution to a problem.

During the field trip, students make their way through the earthquake table exhibit, and I observe them testing their various designs. I encourage them to then revise their original design and test it again. This iterative cycle of test, redesign, and retest represents the basic structure of many engineering and architectural careers and offers a concrete career connection for young children, thus providing additional real-world value to the activity. During one field trip, I observed a student as he stacked objects high on the table; he was using rectangular "floors" and white cylinders to act as "columns" between the floors.

When the student pressed the "earthquake button," causing the table to shake violently, the building quickly toppled over. I asked him, "Why do you think the building fell so quickly?" He answered that the building was "wobbly and really shaky," which he had noticed even before he caused the table to shake. I asked him to take a look at all the materials he had to work with. He found several short plastic rods and began to experiment with how they might fit onto the building. At first, he tried to stack the rods on the bottom of the pile and then tried to attach them to the top of the building. Realizing that he needed some scaffolding, I asked him to look at the picture on the exhibit of the Willis Tower in Chicago. I asked, "Do you notice anything in the picture that you can add to your model?" He took a look at the photograph and exclaimed, "There are Xs between the columns!" He then

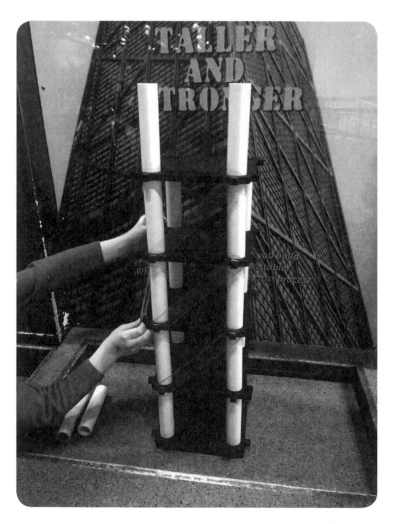

quickly began grabbing the plastic rods and "bracing" each floor diagonally with the rods, emulating the design of the Willis Tower. This redesign step of the technological design process then enabled him to test his revisions.

This time, the tower withstood the "earthquake," and I encouraged my student to make some notes about how the redesign had affected the overall strength of the building. When we returned to class after the field trip, I divided the students into groups and had them talk about the results of their various models and the revisions they had made based on testing. After these group meetings, students imagined that they were architects developing mock presentations for a builder who had hired them to build a skyscraper in an earthquake-prone area. By allowing students to connect this design process to a real-life situation, they gained experience in communicating their ideas in a professional context and made some important career connections in science. Science became relevant through a concrete, real-life application.

 ## How can we make science relevant to the lives of young children?

Connect science to students' present lives

Science is literally all around us, but children often need to be reminded of this fact. In science, it is critical that we help students see the connection between the science that they study in school and their day-to-day lives. Some topics naturally lend themselves to making this connection easily. For example, it's not particularly challenging to connect a study of the five senses to a child's daily experiences. We all taste. We all use our sense of touch. Connection made. However, other topics in science are a bit more challenging. I recall teaching my first-graders a lesson on erosion, specifically on how the movement of water can change the earth's surface. Now, in my experience, kids aren't exactly bouncing off the walls in their excitement to study patterns of erosion. So I had to reach a little deeper to make a connection to the students' daily lives. We took a walk out to the playground. We had recently had a ton of rain, and the water had washed away some dirt at the entrance to the playground, requiring us to "leap" over the trench in the ground. I pointed out that erosion had affected our daily journey to the playground since we now had to be careful not to tumble into the newly formed ditch. Going the extra mile to connect science content to students' daily lives can increase students' value for science and positively affect their motivation for learning science (Eccles and Wigfield 2002).

Connect science to students' future lives

Several years ago, I conducted a research study with children in which I asked them to talk about how science was relevant to their future (Smart 2014). The most common responses were as follows: *I need good grades in science to get into college. I need good grades in science so I can play sports. I need to learn science so I can graduate from high school.* Not one single mention of careers, health, or other practical applications of science in their future lives. The results of this study were eye-opening for me; we simply aren't being explicit enough in educating our students about how science will affect them in the future. Interestingly, this study was conducted in a state that has enacted legislation requiring teachers to connect curriculum to career applications. The Education and Economic Development Act (EEDA) has the goal of helping students make these connections. But something was still getting lost in translation. It is my conclusion that we need to do a much better job of explicitly showing children what science looks like in an adult world. In addition to careers, which is the obvious first thought, science impacts our lives in our ability to evaluate the viability of news reports on scientific topics, interpret the weather forecast, make good decisions for our personal health, and take care of the world around us. Children are not able to draw these conclusions alone; they simply lack the foresight to see twenty years down the road. We must connect the dots for them and in the process strengthen students' understanding of the value of science for their futures.

Bring in science professionals to whom students can relate

One additional element of making science relevant to students' lives is to expose them to professional role models to whom they can relate. It may be more difficult to find female engineers, but little girls need to see that this is a career in which they are represented. Hispanic students need to meet Hispanic doctors. African American students need to hear from African American geologists. When students can imagine themselves having a career in science fields, the world begins to open up to them. I will never forget a personal experience I had as a second-grader in the 1980s. I wanted to be a doctor when I grew up, so for career dress-up day, my mom helped me find a white, button-up coat, and I wore my play stethoscope around my neck. When I got to school, all the other girls in my class were dressed like ballerinas, nurses, teachers—all traditionally female occupations. I remember feeling so out of place, like I had chosen the wrong career to aspire to. At that point in my life, I had never even met a female doctor, since my own pediatrician was a male. What a difference it would have made to meet a woman who had achieved the dream I could only imagine as a seven-year-old. Providing relevant role models in science is a first step to supporting students on their own career journeys.

CHAPTER ELEVEN
Take Cover!

How can we accumulate meaningful resources for our science instruction?

One Sunday afternoon I was cuddled up in my favorite chair reading a book and enjoying a rare moment of relaxation. Courtesy of our modern life with children, those moments are quite rare! Rain softly tapped at my window, and thunder rumbled softly in the distance. As I was nodding off to sleep, an earth-shattering BOOM jolted me back to reality. As I slowly confirmed that nothing in the house had exploded, I began to search for the source of the explosion I had just heard. When I looked out the window, I found the smoking gun . . . or in this case the smoking tree. Lightning had struck the tree outside my bedroom and stripped every inch of bark from its trunk. The tree was steaming, and as we walked outside, the smell of burnt wood filled the air. The bark from the tree was scattered all over our backyard; the tree had literally exploded. Take a look . . .

While my husband debated whether to call the fire department (the tree was still actively smoking), I did what most people would do . . . I started taking pictures! Now you may think I was planning to post the photos on social media or use them to document the incident for insurance purposes should the large, unstable tree fall on our house or light the entire neighborhood on fire. But this would be incorrect. I was planning a science lesson. In truth, I'm always planning a lesson in my head, looking for the perfect picture, story, or example to capture and use to demonstrate a concept to my science students. When you're striving to be an excellent teacher, your planning doesn't stop at a square in your lesson plan book. It follows you home, to the beach, to the mountains, or anywhere that could spark an idea or inspire the collection of a resource to use with your class.

Several weeks after the tree incident, we had one of the most intense hailstorms I have ever experienced. I wish I could show you the video I took of the hail pulverizing our babysitter's new car, which was parked in our driveway . . . it was tragic. (And thankfully covered by insurance!) As soon as the hail stopped falling and it was safe to go outside, I was in our yard with a bowl collecting hailstones. Why? Well, to freeze and use for a science lesson of course! Take a look at these resources for a future unit on severe weather that more or less fell right into my hands! (No pun intended.)

Scientific materials and resources are all around us. The best ones come from our personal experiences and are saved for teachable moments. When lightning hit our tree and when the hailstones fell, I didn't have a unit on severe weather on the horizon, but I filed these resources away for the future. Teaching science is a process that requires constant attention to detail with an eye toward student learning. It requires us to look at the world through a different lens, a lens that values everyday items and experiences as an opportunity to make science relevant and engaging to our students. Below are some suggestions on how to capture your own experiences and collect authentic resources as you continually plan for your science instruction.

How can we accumulate meaningful resources for our science instruction?

Keep a journal

Keeping a journal has always been a practice that I have followed during my years of teaching. I journal about all sorts of things, but this journal is also where I record experiences related to science. When I traveled to Italy, I wrote several journal entries about the way in which Reggio schools teach concepts about light and sound to children. Keeping a journal also allows me to sketch pictures if I am in a place where photography is not allowed. Recently I visited a museum where I wasn't permitted to take photographs. This museum had a geology exhibit focusing on fossils with elements that I wanted to duplicate in my science instruction. Although I wasn't able to photograph them, a simple sketch and a few diagrams in my journal allowed me to capture the essence of those resources for later reference. Since I organize most of my teaching resources electronically, I scanned the sketches from the museum and saved the PDF file for future use. While 3-D resources have to be organized differently, I find it efficient to scan and save PDF copies of journal entries or sketches that I want to reference in the future.

Carry your camera . . . everywhere

This is a no-brainer since no one leaves home without a smartphone these days. When I first started teaching, we were still in the stone age of cameras that required film that had to be developed at a photo studio or darkroom. I'll never forget the time I thought I had beautifully captured a photo of a rare luna moth that landed on my back deck, only to realize after the film was developed that I had taken a picture of my finger! Thankfully, we now live in an era where it's possible to snap quick pictures on our smartphones, send the images to our e-mail, and save them to our computers. These images, however, can easily become buried in the thousands of other pictures on your phone and become inaccessible when you need them. When I capture an image that I can envision using in a future science lesson, I immediately e-mail it to myself and then save it to a folder called "Science Pics." It is also helpful to find these pictures later if you name them with a science concept in mind. For example, I named the photo of the tree struck by lightning "Severe Weather tree" so that I could easily find it at a later date.

Keep a gallon Ziploc in your bag or car

You never know when you're going to find something really cool (and potentially messy) for your science resource collection. Carrying a gallon Ziploc bag with you at all times ensures that you will have a safe, mess-free method of preserving your find. For example, a few years ago, my children and I were having a picnic beside a lake, and we found an abandoned bird nest on the ground. I pulled my science Ziploc bag from my purse and in went the bird nest. That's not exactly the sort of thing you want to stuff in a diaper bag . . . mites, you know. I have three plastic crates for my science "finds," labeled Life Science, Physical Science, and Earth Science. The bird nest went into the Life Science crate and emerged last month during a lesson I taught to my son's preschool class on birds. If you follow the Boy Scouts motto and plan to "be prepared," you won't miss out on the fantastic (yet potentially unsanitary) science resources that might unexpectedly cross your path.

Collect people as resources

People are the most valuable resource you can collect for your science instruction. Just as you are preparing to collect resources in many forms in your daily life, you need to plan to collect people. Now I'm obviously not suggesting that you kidnap someone in the grocery line—the police would likely frown on that. I'm talking about developing a network of science experts from your community that you can "tap" for their knowledge and expertise. For example, I once met a chemist in the line at the bank and later had her come in to do some simple experiments with my class when we were studying phase changes in matter. Now I have to admit that I'm the type who can strike up a conversation with a wall—it's one of those traits that we southerners are known for. So what if you're not comfortable striking up conversations with complete strangers? There are many other ways to network with the professionals in your area. Consider joining community organizations (e.g., neighborhood associations), attending public forums, participating in special-interest groups (e.g., recreational sports leagues, gardening clubs, nonprofit organizations), and volunteering in your community. The goal is to put yourself in situations where you might meet potential science resources right in your own community. In my experience, local citizens in science-related fields have been extremely willing to share their expertise with my classes. Many commented that they had never been asked before and were excited for the opportunity. Another option for "collecting" people resources is becoming involved with professional organizations for science teachers. Most states have a chapter of the National Science Teachers Association with an annual meeting geared toward bringing teachers together with science professionals. These meetings are an excellent place to make professional connections for your classroom. Even if these individuals don't live in a convenient location to visit your school, you can utilize technologies such as Skype and FaceTime to have them make a virtual visit to your classroom. Building a strong network of people resources with specific areas of scientific expertise can strengthen the content you are able to offer your students and can also serve as a learning opportunity to strengthen your own science content knowledge.

CHAPTER TWELVE
Playing with Fire

How can we ensure safety for all children during science instruction?

I wish I could lie and say that this chapter title is a play on words. It isn't. I actually set my classroom on fire once. Thankfully, I was able to quickly extinguish the fire and avoid any dire outcomes, but it scared me to death. The fire incident occurred during my first year of teaching as a result of a demonstration gone horribly wrong. Ironically, we were in the middle of a unit on fire safety. Let that sink in for a minute. I wanted to show my students that a fire could survive only if it had oxygen and that a flame could be extinguished by cutting off its oxygen supply. I set up a table at the front of the room with a candle and a tall glass. I lit the candle and was about the cover the candle with the glass to demonstrate this principle. As I lifted the glass in my hand, however, I somehow managed to lose my grip and the glass fell onto the desk, knocking the candle off the table and *onto the carpet*. Now, let me stop for a moment and point out that this is likely why carpet has been ripped out of most schools. Linoleum doesn't catch fire. In case you are wondering, carpet does. Quickly. The candle hit the carpet and immediately set the entire floor on fire. The next few moments were a blur. I yelled at my students to go out the back patio of our classroom (thankfully we had an outdoor exit), and I grabbed the fire extinguisher from the closet. Within a few seconds, I had extinguished the fire, and our room was covered in a white powder that smelled horrible. I immediately called my principal, and we set about restoring order to the classroom and assuring the students that everything would be OK. A single candle had taught me just how quickly science can get dangerous. The unexpected can happen in a moment and blindside you completely. That day transformed me into a champion for safety in the science classroom and convinced me to revamp the way I plan for science lessons.

As teachers, we have no choice but to imagine and then plan for the worst. I now try to envision every possible hazard to safety and then make a proactive plan to avoid it. But even with intense planning, accidents can still happen. For example, during a unit on science process skills, I gave each student a bag of seashells and instructed everyone to classify shells into groups with similar characteristics. While the students were working, a shell broke and cut a huge gash into a young girl's hand. By definition, an accident is something that you could not reasonably foresee. This is different from a safety hazard, which would be a likely and predictable result of an activity. Lighting a candle over a carpeted floor is a safety hazard; handing a student a bag of seashells is not. See the difference? We cannot eliminate our science instruction from all risk, but we can plan ahead to avoid safety hazards and have protocols in place to respond quickly to accidents.

How can we ensure safety for all children during science instruction?

Develop a safety contract with your students

During the first week of school, teachers should develop a safety contract with their students and have all students sign the contract. This document should explain how you expect students to act during science activities and outline acceptable behaviors and unacceptable behaviors while *doing* science. Students should also be made aware of the consequences of breaking this safety contract. A copy should be sent home to parents, and a copy should be placed in each student's file. This contract encourages accountability during science activities and develops a classroom community that values safety. On several occasions, I have had students blatantly violate their safety contracts by refusing to follow directions. I walk over to my filing cabinet, pull out the safety contract that the child has previously signed, and inform the child that she will not be participating in further science activities until she can hold up her side of the contract. I then send the contract home with the child with a note explaining to the parents how their child has repeatedly broken the contract, and we set up a conference to make a plan for the future. Nine times out of ten, this process yields the results I am seeking: a safe science classroom. In that rare exception, I haven't hesitated to get my administration involved to ensure each student abides by the contract we have developed to keep the science classroom a safe place. The implementation of a safety contract is also a good real-world example for children of agreements they will need to sign in other areas of their life when they are older. Appendix G provides a sample science safety contract for elementary grades as well as a simplified version for early childhood grades.

Create a safe place to do science

There are many safety precautions that you can take to ensure that your classroom is a safe environment for children to conduct scientific investigations. It may seem surprising that you need to take these precautions at an early childhood or elementary level (this is obviously not a high school

chemistry course, right?). But there are still some common safety measures that you need to take to protect yourself and your students. You always need to be able to prove that you took all realistic measures to avoid an accident on your watch.

The following is a list of safety materials that you should have in your classroom:

- goggles
- lockable cabinet for science materials and tools
- fire extinguisher
- sand
- nonglass containers
- safety posters
- water source
- first aid kit

The following is a list of safety materials that students should have access to in the classroom:

- extra T-shirts or lab coats (for messy investigations)
- scissors (instead of blades)
- cleanup materials
- rubber gloves (not latex, due to allergies)

This basic list of materials can help you proactively plan to make your class-room a safe place for your students to explore science. As you build your collection of science resources, you may discover additional materials that you would like to have available, but this is a good start.

Document. Document. Document.

This is excellent advice for a teacher in general but especially when teaching science. Documentation is an absolute must. Your first step to documenting your safety is to complete the science contracts discussed earlier. These are proof that you have covered science safety with your students and also have informed parents of the expectations in your classroom. Another important source of documentation in science is your lesson plans. Your lesson plans are a legal document. Use your plans to record each specific safety lesson you teach to each class as well as safety details specific to individual lessons. In addition, create a file in which you store any and all documentation of science-related injuries (no matter how minor), safety quizzes, and contact with parents. If an issue goes to court, the following is considered the legal litmus test for safety situations: Would another reasonable and competent professional teacher have done the same thing in the same situation? Documentation is something you hope you will never need, but it is too important to bypass.

Know the children in your class

We all have "one of those classes." You know, the class you were afraid to turn your back on for five seconds. If you are dealing with a class that includes children who routinely exhibit unpredictable and erratic behavior, it's best to put the hot plates away for the year. This is where common sense comes in. If in doubt, err on the side of caution, and find an alternate method for teaching the concept at hand. This doesn't mean nixing scientific inquiry completely (see chapter 13) but minimizing the potential safety risks of the activities you plan. If there are demonstrations that you decide are too risky for the classroom, downloading a video clip of the demonstration can be a good consolation prize. And it is definitely cheaper than a lawsuit.

CHAPTER THIRTEEN
Swimming in the Deep End

How can we meet the needs of all students in science instruction?

I once taught a child who stabbed me with a pencil, breaking the whole lead tip off in my arm. That wasn't a stellar day. Through the years, I have taught some challenging kiddos, but this child stands out among all the others. (We all have one, don't we?) Aaron taught me how to swim in the deep end, often while holding a large boulder. (Names have been changed to protect the innocent, of course.) Aaron came into class each day with a chip on his shoulder. No one could blame him; he had lived through more in his seven years than most of us can imagine. He battled anger and rage and confusion that goes beyond what any child should have to bear. I must preface everything in this chapter with the following words: I loved Aaron dearly. But an easy year, it was not.

Because of the severity of Aaron's behavior, I found myself changing the entire direction of my teaching to ensure that things would go "smoothly." In particular, I made many adjustments to my science curriculum to remove any ambiguity and possibilities for disaster. I had always prided myself on doing active, engaging activities with my students in which they got to experience the science they were studying, not just read about it. However, the amount of structure that was required to manage Aaron's behavior just didn't "fit" with many hands-on, active learning experiences in science—at least that was my disposition at the time.

One Friday, we were watching a Bill Nye video at the conclusion of
an earth science unit. A scientist on the show was demonstrating how to
make a volcano erupt with a mixture of vinegar and baking soda. One of
my students looked over at me and said, "Mrs. Smart, why don't we ever do
anything exciting like that in science? I want science to be fun like that." It
broke my heart. In an effort to control the classroom environment and main-
tain order, I had sucked the life and love out of my favorite subject in the
curriculum. I decided then and there that things had to change. I simply had
to challenge myself to reintroduce student-centered science instruction into
my class while taking Aaron's behavioral needs into consideration. Along
with the rest of the class, he deserved to love and enjoy science too.

Since my class had been so impressed with Bill Nye's volcano, I decided
that was a great starting point for our inquiry adventures. That weekend
I pored over research literature on engaging children with emotional and
behavioral disorders (EBD) in hands-on learning experiences. One of the
themes that kept emerging was the need for students with EBD to have a
well-defined role in the activity that would allow them to direct their focus
onto a specific task, thereby decreasing the likelihood of off-task behavior
(i.e., acting out). As I considered the various roles that Aaron could take in
the demonstration, I decided that he would be excellent at photographing
the activity and adding it to our classroom documentation wall. He had
expressed some interest in the digital camera (which at the time were quite
new), and I decided to give it a shot. Yes, I would be taking a bit of a risk by
entrusting an expensive item to a child with highly unpredictable behavior,
but teachers have lots of extra cash to spare, so why not? (insert sarcasm).

On Monday, the class was bubbling with excitement (no pun intended)
when they saw boxes of baking soda, bottles of vinegar, and vials of red food
coloring on my science table. During our morning snack break, I called
Aaron to my desk and asked him if he would like to be the photographer for
our science experiment. I'm sure I will never forget his wide-eyed expression
and the smile that spread across his face when I handed him the camera and
gave him some lessons about the different functions. He looked at me and
asked me a question that is embedded in my heart forever: "Are you sure
you want to trust me with this camera?" I assured him that, yes, I absolutely
wanted to trust him with the job and gave him an assuring thumbs-up. Here

stood before me a child who had been marginalized and "worked around" and fenced off from many opportunities that "normal" children took for granted and was quite skeptical of my trust in him. Now we were about to dive into the deep end and see if we could swim.

When the time came for our science experiment, groups gathered expectantly around their model volcanoes as we mixed materials to cause our controlled eruptions. My anxiety melted as I saw Aaron completely engaged in documenting the work of each group. He ducked under students' elbows and over their notebooks to get the perfect angle of each volcanic eruption and asked students to pose with the foamy aftermath of their experiments. He was a natural. The science activity went off without a hitch, and the next day I put Aaron to work posting the printed pictures of his work on our documentation wall. From that day forward, Aaron earned the title of "Classroom Documentation Specialist" (fancy, huh?) and continued to photograph many aspects of our classroom life. I wish I could say that every day was perfect and that Aaron never had another earth-shattering outburst, but that wouldn't be true. We had difficult days. We had better days. But we were *doing* science again, and Aaron had found his place in the mix. And on our toughest days, I knew what would motivate Aaron through his outbursts. "I need my photographer, Aaron," I would say. "We need this documented." And many times it got us through what would have otherwise been catastrophic outbursts. I resolved to never again alter my teaching philosophy because of my perceived limitations of any student. Because in the end, my perceptions turned out to be wrong. Every child *can* do science and has the right to experience it in an engaging, meaningful way. It's not easy, but it's worth it. Just ask Aaron.

How can we meet the needs of all learners during science instruction?

Differentiate instruction through open-ended activities

In the modern science classroom, you will likely be teaching children representing a wide range of cognitive abilities. Inquiry-based instruction has the potential to be implemented effectively with all learners, from your lowest-ability group to your most gifted learner. The manner in which instruction is delivered and scaffolded is critical to differentiating instruction in order to reach all ability levels (Tomlinson 2014). The nature of inquiry-based instruction incorporates the use of open-ended questions during science. One of the benefits of posing open-ended questions for students to explore is that it inherently allows students to work at their own level. A gifted student can approach a problem by adding an additional level of complexity, while students with lower cognitive abilities can also access the same science at their own level. For example, in a classroom where students are studying safety in severe weather, the teacher may pose the following open-ended question to students: How can you stay safe at home during a tornado? The teacher may then provide a variety of sources on different levels for students to research this question, and students can then communicate their ideas at their own level of proficiency. Through this open format, teachers are able to differentiate their level of questioning and support depending on the needs of the students. At the same time, students are not locked into a specific closed format that limits the ability levels that can be expressed simultaneously.

Differentiate instruction through rich classroom discussions

In addition, inquiry-based instruction allows students to take an active part in the discussion of scientific ideas; this format enables the teacher to hear student ideas and truly understand the level of understanding of each student. As a result, the teacher can direct the lesson to address ideas that multiple students are struggling to grasp. Differentiation through classroom discussion requires the teacher to use effective questioning to engage students in conversations about science and then use these responses to adjust instruction to make the ideas accessible to all students. By asking questions on various cognitive levels, the teacher can direct a whole class discussion to target a variety of ability levels. Asking questions ranging from lower-level knowledge questions to higher-level evaluation questions allows all students to access the scientific concept in an appropriate and meaningful way. In addition, student responses give teachers valuable information about which students may benefit from more focused, individualized instruction on the topic.

In addition, class discussions provide an opportunity for students to learn from each other. For example, students who have a solid grasp on the content can voice their own ideas, adding a level of peer modeling to the learning process. During inquiry-based instruction, students are encouraged to talk directly to each other to explain concepts in alternative ways; this practice often allows peers to communicate with each other in meaningful ways and makes material more accessible to all students. For example, it was common practice in my third-grade classroom for students to come to the board and attempt to explain a difficult concept to their peers using their own thinking. In addition to helping other students understand the material, the students presenting their ideas are able to operate at a higher cognitive level by explaining and justifying their own thinking. These elements of inquiry-based instruction are natural sources of differentiation by ability level in the science classroom, making science concepts more accessible to all students.

Differentiate instruction by using a wide range of learning modalities

Student-centered instructional approaches, such as inquiry, utilize a wide range of materials, instructional formats, and communication styles so that all children are capable of accessing and representing their ideas in science. The concrete nature of inquiry-based instruction helps all students experience the curriculum in authentic ways and in turn reaches across many of the barriers created by learning disorders, processing disorders, and autism. I once taught a child with Asperger's who was not comfortable communicating verbally with his peers; however, he created rich, beautiful paintings of his scientific ideas to share with the class. Inquiry's emphasis on communicating ideas in a variety of ways and mediums lends itself naturally to providing all learners with a way to express their learning.

Differentiate instruction by varying the scaffolding of activities

Inquiry-based instruction can vary widely in the amount of structure given to activities and experiments. Student-centered instruction can still be meaningful and accomplish its primary goals in a more structured environment. Sometimes we teach a group of students who thrive in self-directed settings; sometimes we don't. If you have a class that includes many children who need a high level of structure in the day, don't throw inquiry out the window. As demonstrated in my story about Aaron, science can still include engaging, active elements, even if you are dealing with behavioral challenges or specific learning needs that require a more structured approach. It is possible to implement effective inquiry by preserving the essence of the activity and placing additional supports to make the science accessible to all students. One way to do this is to increase the amount of scaffolding for the activity (Vygotsky 1978). For example, if students are completing an activity on sorting animals into groups by similar physical characteristics, you may incorporate additional guiding questions while students are working instead of having them sort all of the animals independently. Additional scaffolding can also be provided by changing the context of an activity; for example, an activity initially designed to be completed by small groups could be completed as a whole class with individual students taking turns completing steps of the process. While we want students to work at their most independent level possible, science activities can be adapted to a whole group experience if necessary. In other words, when additional scaffolding is needed, we don't need to default to work sheets to access a specific science activity. Instead we can adapt the activity to our specific needs, preserving the essence of the activity.

CHAPTER FOURTEEN

When the Train Derails

How do we respond to unexpected challenges during science instruction?

It was Monday. It was one of *those* Mondays. You know the days I'm talking about, when it's amazing you even *made* it to the science lesson at all. As my little tykes squirmed and bounced around on the rug, I secretly wondered how we were going to get through this lesson and actually manage to infuse some scientific meaning into these young brains. We were working through a unit on animal adaptations, and the focus of the present lesson was camouflage. I began by showing my students a picture of a yellow snake camouflaged in some yellow sand. Almost immediately, a scream erupted from my class; Addie had burst into tears and was informing anyone within ear's reach that she was deathly afraid of snakes and could not *even* be in the same room with one. It took several minutes to calm Addie down and convince her that I had not in fact brought a real poisonous snake into our classroom (I was anticipating an interesting parent phone call later in the day to clear this point up.). My lesson was officially *off* the tracks. Any hope of activating children's prior knowledge about animal camouflage and directing their brains to begin thinking about the subject at hand had just derailed with the emotional outburst. So, we collectively gathered ourselves, and I forged ahead to the next activity in the lesson.

At each student's table, dozens of tiny, cutout butterflies were sitting meticulously against a background resembling a patch of dirt. (Yes, they actually make scrapbooking paper that looks like dirt! Who knew!) Half of the butterflies were bright colors, and half were cut from the same "dirt pattern" as the background so they would blend in, making them harder to find. This lesson was getting back on track, and I was feeling pretty good as I admired the delicate butterflies that I had stayed up until midnight preparing the night before. As students pretended to be birds and "hunt" for the butterflies, I questioned them about their "hunting." They responded with focused comments such as, "These bright butterflies are easier to see!" and "Why is it so hard to find the brown ones?"

The teacher in me glowed as my students were experiencing the concept of camouflage in action. Then, it happened. Almost as if I was watching in slow motion, I saw a student with a mischievous grin on her face inhale a huge breath of air and then blow it out all across her table. Butterflies flew everywhere. It was like a paper snowstorm as butterflies landed all across the floor. Students erupted in laughter, and one quipped, "Look! I can see all the butterflies now! They weren't really hiding!" *Off* the tracks again. I tried to regroup everyone and make the point that the *reason* the brown butterflies were visible now was because they were on a different surface (i.e., the white tile floor). However, that leap in logic was a bit too developmentally sophisticated for my four-year-olds, and the activity quickly descended into dramatic reenactments of the butterfly catastrophe.

As we moved back to the rug to try to retain some semblance of meaning from the lesson, I decided to go back to square one. I quickly rehearsed in my mind the main idea that my students needed to walk away with that particular day: animals can survive by blending in with the area around them. With a little reworking, our extension activity could still accomplish this goal. Originally, I had planned an elaborate hide-and-seek game in which students would design their own butterflies to "camouflage" in their classroom environment while the other students took turns hunting for them. However, after the complications with the earlier portions of the lesson, I needed more focus and structure to get this lesson firmly back on track and accomplish my learning objectives. I still retained the original extension activity and had each student study our classroom and color their butterfly so that it could "hide" and stay safe from a hungry bird. Instead of a potentially unfocused hide-and-seek game, however, I gave the students the chance to present their butterfly to the class and explain where the butterfly would be hiding and why. This more structured approach allowed me to listen closely to each student's current level of understanding regarding camouflage and to interject some scaffolding as needed. For example, some students had actually absorbed more than I had previously expected. Noah colored his butterfly red and "hid" it on a red poster in our classroom. Claire colored her butterfly pink and camouflaged it against a pink coat in the cubbies.

There were blue butterflies hiding on our blue rug and even a polka-dotted butterfly seeking refuge in our polka-dotted curtains. This was good. This was promising. However, there were multiple students who needed various levels of scaffolding to support their developing concept of camouflage. Lana colored her butterfly purple and orange and tried to place it on the white wall. I asked her, "Lana, if you were a bird, would you be able to see that butterfly really well?" She agreed that a bird would likely see the butterfly pretty easily. Using guiding questions, I followed up with, "Let's look around the room for a place that has the same colors as your butterfly so it won't be as easy to find." Together, we walked around and found a poster of a rainbow where the butterfly could be better concealed and hopefully avoid becoming bluebird breakfast.

How Do We Respond to Unexpected Challenges during Science Instruction?

Stay the course

Throughout this particular lesson, there were plenty of opportunities to lose track of the original intent of the lesson and completely miss the learning objectives for my students. Many lessons require us to fend off distractions, unexpected interruptions, atypical student responses, and just a general slew of unavoidable external influences (Harris and Rooks 2010). At the core of each lesson are the objectives that should be guiding us every step of the way. They are our final destination. The lesson we originally plan represents just one possible path toward achieving this goal and arriving at the intended destination. We have to be willing to go "off the beaten path" to get our students to the destination. If we can retain our focus when things don't go as planned, we can regroup and still salvage the original intent of the lesson. Even if a particular activity doesn't play out the way we had intended, we can still keep the lesson on course and finish strong. In the camouflage lesson, once the first butterfly activity flopped, we quickly regrouped and got back to the focus of the lesson—camouflage. It wasn't butterflies that we were focusing on anyway; the activity was merely the context in which we were studying a much larger concept. So keeping an eye on the horizon and charting a new path to get you to your final destination is the first key when responding to unexpected events in your science classroom.

Adjust. Adapt. Accept.

I had a choral director in college who took our group on many international tours. When we encountered the unavoidable challenge while on the road (e.g., lost luggage, malfunctioning sound equipment, jet lag), he would simply repeat the following: "Adjust. Adapt. Accept." We were to make necessary adjustments, adapt to our unexpected circumstances, and, most importantly, *accept* them. As teachers we are asked to make adjustments to our instructional plan daily (I once had to *literally* throw my lesson plans out because a student threw up on them!). Effective teaching occurs when we meet these challenges with resolve and make real-time adjustments to meet the learning needs of our students. Most importantly, we have to *accept* these unexpected challenges. This is especially difficult for me; I am a type A personality to the core! I spent hours cutting out those tiny butterflies! I wanted that activity to go perfectly! But I would not have served my students or myself by coming unglued when things didn't go as planned. Sure, I secretly wanted to have a mini-meltdown and go to Starbucks for the rest of the day, but I chose to adjust, adapt, accept. And somehow, through the derailments and the rerouting, my students arrived at their destination. Granted, the train was a little dented and beat-up when we arrived, but we got there.

Learn from it, and plan for the future

Some of the best, most effective lessons in my repertoire didn't start out that way. Many of these lessons that run so smoothly in the present originated from lessons that completely failed on the first (or even second and third) attempts. But I chose not to throw the baby out with the bathwater; I believed in the potential of the lesson, and I kept revising until I got it right. I have a personal practice of journaling for a few minutes after problematic lessons. For one, it helps me to channel my anxiety in a positive way, and it also helps me to learn from my mistakes. Teaching is an art form that takes decades to perfect; most retired teachers will tell you they were still making changes in their practice after twenty-five years in the classroom! As I journal about lessons that have not gone particularly well, I ask myself a series of questions: What went right? (There's always some glimmer of hope!), What didn't go as I planned? and What can I change the next time I teach this lesson? Do you notice all of the "I" language in those questions? It's intentional. There is a concept in educational psychology called "locus of control," and it pertains to the attributions we make when things go wrong (Weiner 2005). It is much healthier when we can attribute the lesson's failure to something in our own control. For example, *I* can manage my materials differently next time. *I* can pace the lesson differently next time. *I* can add more scaffolds to the lesson in the future. This type of language places the locus of control firmly in our own court and provides us with confidence that we can be successful in the future.

CHAPTER FIFTEEN
Creepy-Crawlies

How can we model positive attitudes about science for children?

Nothing gets me screaming like a hissing cockroach! Honestly, how many times do you get to utter that sentence in your lifetime? I guess I need to provide a little context: I hate creepy-crawlies. I shiver at the thought of little wiggling bugs getting anywhere near me, and I don't hide it well. So imagine my "joy" when our class attended a special field trip featuring, you guessed it, bugs. And it wasn't enough for us to just examine the bugs from afar, observing them behind glass and in cages (very secure, I hoped); no, we were going to get to hold them too! Yay! (Note forced enthusiasm.)

We are lucky to be in a school district with a fantastic science center. Classes are routinely treated to amazing science lessons both at the science center and at our own school via remote learning opportunities. On this field trip, my class had signed up for an interactive life science experience focused on mammals and reptiles. Apparently, the brochure forgot to mention the hissing cockroaches, a "bonus" thrown in just for us! Our class had already been treated to a wonderful session that included passing around and feeling animals, such as a chinchilla, a boa constrictor, several small geckos, and even a field mouse. I feel the need to point out that I joyously held the boa constrictor, even allowing the scaly fella to coil around my neck and give me a little "love squeeze" (still not sure that squeeze was grounded in love). So I was feeling pretty proud of being the cool, collected teacher until the field guide announced that we had a final, surprise guest. And out came the hissing cockroaches.

As soon as I laid eyes on those cockroaches, my skin started to crawl. As the field guide selected me to go first to hold one of the special friends, I wish I could say that I bravely conquered my fear and set an amazing example for my young charges. But that wasn't what happened. Instead I responded by leaping backwards away from the bug and knocking over a chair, tripping over the chair, and falling to the floor. Nice. I had just modeled my irrational fear of cockroaches for my students, and they took notice. Not one of them would hold the hissing cockroach after my embarrassing display. Not one.

We do this all the time in subtle ways, don't we? We pass along our attitudes and dispositions toward science to our students. Maybe it's not quite as dramatic as knocking over chairs to get away from a hissing cockroach, but we often communicate our feelings toward science to our children through our words, actions, and responses. Research shows that many teachers had negative personal experiences with science, either as young children who found science boring or irrelevant, or as college students who struggled to pass chemistry. Those attitudes are deeply engrained in us. Negative attitudes translate into actions and words that communicate those feelings to our students. A subtle, seemingly harmless comment like "I wasn't good at science" and deciding to casually bump the science lesson to the last waning minutes of the school day both send negative messages about science.

How can we model positive attitudes about science to children?

Acknowledge your own attitudes about science

The first step in modeling positive attitudes about science is to acknowledge our own personal dispositions (Tobias and Everson 2002). Let's face it, many of us did not have the best experiences in science as students. There may be real, legitimate reasons for the negative feelings you may have about specific areas of science. Personally, I was fortunate to have a lot of great early experiences with science . . . then came organic chemistry. Have you ever met an obstacle that just seemed insurmountable? For me, that was the semester that I encountered organic chemistry and began to question my dreams of becoming an epidemiologist. All throughout high school, my career goal was to work as a research scientist for the Centers for Disease Control and Prevention. I could envision no career more fascinating than one that required me to spend my days combating all sorts of viruses, diseases, and plagues. Then I hit a tremendous pothole in the road to this dream. As I struggled through organic chemistry, I spent countless nights poring over chemical equations and formulas, but the subject matter just wouldn't stick. Though I ultimately passed the class, this was an experience that decimated my self-efficacy and confidence in chemistry. My struggles with organic chemistry ultimately led me to pursue a different career path; the effects of this negative experience, however, would linger and resurface years later.

Five years later I was in my own classroom, teaching physical science to fourth-graders. One day, a student came up to me after class and asked me a surprising question. He said, "Do you like chemistry?" I offered a teacherly answer, "Of course! Why do you ask?" The student replied, "Well, you just don't seem very excited about it. You're always excited about science, and I can tell you don't like this as much." I was astonished that somehow my negative experiences with chemistry years ago had seeped into my teaching. This forced me to take a deep look at myself and acknowledge that I still harbored negative feelings toward this content area and had subconsciously allowed these attitudes to color my teaching. Simply reflecting on my true feelings about chemistry prompted me to make some adjustments in my teaching. I realized that I was less likely to plan engaging lab experiences for this area of my science instruction, possibly because they reminded me of my miserable days in the organic chemistry laboratory (Those labs could last six to eight hours at a time!). I began taking inventory of my own hang-ups in science and "plugging the holes" where I had allowed those hang-ups to spill over into my own instruction.

Be mindful of the language you use during science

Words are powerful. As teachers, we have a platform unlike any other in society. Young, impressionable minds are actively absorbing our ideas every day during a key developmental period in their lives. Now, I'm sure there are days you're convinced that your students aren't hearing a word you say. But rest assured . . . they are listening. Once a parent of one of my third-graders remarked, "Mrs. Smart, we *hear* you at home." I thought that was an odd concept at the time, that my words were actually being repeated at children's homes because they had absorbed them and were now using them as their own. I remember feeling a heavy sense of responsibility and wondering, what exactly were the parents *hearing* at home? Now my own children come home with their own teachers' ideas impressed on their tiny brains, and I have a whole new understanding of what it means to *hear* a teacher's voice in the voice of their young students.

When we talk about science in class, our children literally absorb every word and sentiment like sponges, then incorporate our attitudes and feelings into their own worldview. The words we speak, sometimes unintentionally, resonate loudly in the minds of our students. I have spent many hours observing science teachers and have had the opportunity to hear a variety of attitudes relayed during instruction. Some of these have been on the negative side: "This is really hard, and I didn't like it when I was a student"; "Now this isn't fun, but we have to learn it anyway"; "I used to think this was really boring. Let's just plow through it." I kid you not; these are direct quotations from teachers in the classroom. I've even heard some gender-biased speech in science classrooms: "Girls don't usually like this part (i.e., building circuits), but everyone needs to try it." My jaw nearly dropped to the floor in awe during these moments. Now, these teachers didn't intend to communicate these negative attitudes to their students; most of them were equally horrified when we debriefed about their lessons afterwards and we discussed these statements. Sometimes we just don't monitor the type of talk we are using and how it can affect our students. Good teachers communicate negative attitudes unintentionally. The starting point has to be our own mindfulness about the type of statements we make during science instruction (Fried 2001). I routinely take a video of myself teaching to watch for such language. In the same way that we continuously monitor our students, we have to continuously monitor our own language.

Initiate parent education about the power of positive attitudes

In addition to your influence as a teacher, other relationships can exert even greater influence on students and make a lasting impact on their views of science and their ability to succeed in science. The messages that students receive from their parents and other close family members make a dramatic impact on their own attitudes and beliefs. Because of this connection, I make a concerted effort to educate parents about the effect their attitudes have on their children.

In my first school, I taught many children who were the first generation from their families who would go on to graduate from high school. Many of the parents had negative experiences with schooling in general. In one situation, the mother was so anxious about the schooling process that she would not come to teacher-student conferences. I tried to reach out to parents in a way that put their minds at ease about the science that their children were doing at school. I tried to develop simple science activities that my students could do with their parents to provide positive experiences for both child and parent. For example, I sent home seeds and potting soil for our plants unit and asked the children to plant a small garden with their families. I had my students make sketches of the garden and also asked for parents to do a few sketches as well. One student returned his sketches one day and said, "My mom and I had fun planting the seeds, and she said it was the first time she liked science!" This was the reason I had initiated this level of parental involvement: to provide a positive experience not only for the student but for the family as well.

As the school year progresses, I try to plan a few small science demonstrations for parents to attend. I want them to feel welcome in my classroom and to have an opportunity to participate in some of the science we are doing together. Any time that I can get a parent into my classroom, I have an opportunity to model positive science "talk" for them and also have a chance to get to know them on a deeper level. When I am able to identify parents with a skill that we can incorporate into my science instruction, I love to have them teach the students. In addition to providing another adult role model for my students, the parents also gain confidence in their own abilities to contribute in a positive way to our science learning. All of these factors combine to set the stage for more positive science experiences for my students, resulting in more positive attitudes about science.

CHAPTER SIXTEEN
On the Road Again . . .

How can we maximize the learning potential of field trips in science?

Never take first-graders to the zoo in the spring-time. Just trust me on this one. Love is in the air in the animal kingdom during the spring months, and as a first-year teacher it was definitely not something I was prepared to address with wide-eyed six-year-olds. One cool April morning, I naively loaded up a bus of first-graders for a trip to the zoo in our city. All of the children were sporting their new bright-yellow class T-shirts and freshly printed name tags. My chaperones had all arrived early, and we were busy collecting lunch boxes and loading up our first aid kit, snacks, sunscreen, treats for the ride home, and even some chewing gum for one student who got very motion sick. I was ready. No teacher could have been more ready than I was.

My students were on their best behavior all the way to the zoo as they happily sang songs and bounced up and down with excitement. I had my coffee in hand and was feeling pretty confident. Yep, I was nailing this field trip thing. I should have had a clue when we got to the zoo and saw that we were the only school group there. Seriously, this place looked like a ghost town except for my sweet, little color-coordinated angels. We decided to start with the monkey exhibit, and all the children eagerly crowded around to get a better view. And did we ever get a view. I panicked as I saw the monkeys getting well acquainted with each other. *Very* well acquainted. The chaperones and I tried to herd the children away from the amorous monkeys as students protested, making many curious remarks such as, "Why were the monkeys wrestling?" and "Those monkeys must be best friends!" I was already anticipating the parent phone calls and e-mails that evening. We quickly recovered and walked through the reptile house, which was much less eventful, thankfully. I was feeling good about the day again until we rounded the corner and arrived at the tiger exhibit. You guessed it . . . the tigers were getting well acquainted as well.

I quickly cornered a zoo employee as I sent the children to the safety of the playground. She confirmed that yes, we had indeed chosen to visit the zoo at the peak of mating season. Oops. My bad. We spent the rest of the field trip sending chaperones ahead of the group to "scope out" the current activities at each animal exhibit before we took the children to see each animal. Let's just say that we didn't get to visit the gorillas or the lions that day. Incidentally, this led to a gigantic meltdown by a child who just *had* to see the lions. Not today, Steven. Not today. I literally had to carry this kicking and screaming child to the bus . . . good times. Lesson learned. From that day on, I never planned another field trip without doing a significant amount of research on every aspect of the location, timing, and possible pitfalls. And we always visited the zoo during the safe and much-less-active fall months. Turns out that romance takes a major dive in the animal world as the weather cools. Thank goodness.

How can we maximize the learning potential of field trips in science?

Do your homework

When planning ahead, it is crucial to do your homework. Whenever I can, I like to visit the field trip site before taking my class. Is that always possible? No. Are you paid for this visit? Not usually. Does it pay dividends in knowing how to logistically plan for the trip? Absolutely. If an actual visit to the site is not possible, call and speak with someone at the location to find out the schedule for the day and to request any materials that may help in preparing your students for the trip. If this is your first time taking students to this location, talk to other teachers who've been on this field trip with students, and ask for advice about the pros and cons of the experience. If you consistently receive negative feedback from other teachers about the experience, look for an alternative. Keep in mind that many science resources will come to you. Some examples are traveling gem-mining facilities, animal handlers, and inflatable planetariums. Though off-campus field trips are more traditional, bringing science resources to you can often provide the same quality experience with less cost and easier logistics.

Get organized, and enlist help

During your planning for a field trip, it is important to identify the specific connections of the field trip to your science standards and curriculum. Field trips usually offer a wide array of information and experiences, and it is up to you as the teacher to determine the focus of the experience during the planning phase. If you are touring a large aquarium, for example, take time in advance to plan the path that your students will take through the exhibits, making sure to include those that are the most developmentally appropriate and align best with your science curriculum. In other words, if your kindergarteners have the opportunity to visit a farm and you have been studying the life cycle of plants, save the corn maze for last, and head straight to the apple orchard to make those science connections early before they get too tired. Taking the time to plan the most effective itinerary is especially important when planning field trips for young children, who tire easily and have short attention spans.

Prep your students

When taking students on a field trip, an effective practice is to prepare them for what they will see and learn on the trip. I like to give my students a focus question to think about or an activity to keep them focused during the trip. For example, second-grade standards in our state require students to be able to classify animals by their physical characteristics. In planning a zoo field trip, it would be appropriate to develop a scavenger hunt for students to complete as they tour the zoo in which they have to find animals with similar physical characteristics. Present the items on the scavenger hunt to the class before the trip, and have adult chaperones carry a short list of scavenger hunt items for the children, reminding them to look for these things during the trip. Preparing activities to be completed by students while on the field trip serves to focus students on the science you want them to learn. Such activities don't have to be complicated; think of them as a simple way to emphasize important aspects of the field trip for your students, thus maximizing the information they are likely to absorb and retain.

Document the trip for future reference

Taking pictures during the field trip is an excellent way to help students recall their experiences and allow for class discussion of highlights from the trip. It is now easier than ever to document the field trip with your electronic device and to take short videos to discuss with your students later. I also like to interview my students during the field trip to capture their ideas about what they are seeing and potential questions they have that we can explore once we are back in the classroom. Making a documentation panel about the field trip in the classroom is also a great way to refer back to this common experience, which becomes a reference point as examples for future units in science. You can also allow older children to document the field trip with digital cameras. As a third-grade teacher, I wrote a grant for five digital cameras that could be used by students to document our learning, including experiences on field trips. Communicating ideas in science is a critical process skill; photography can provide a medium for students to share their ideas about science concepts encountered on a field trip.

Plan an extension activity with a science focus

One of the most common post–field trip activities is having students write a story about the trip or illustrate their favorite part. While this can certainly be an effective activity for students to reflect on their experiences, planning specific science-focused activities to follow up on a field trip can help to extend students' understanding of key science concepts. For example, following a gem-mining field trip, children kept their gems and rocks at school for a week and completed specific activities focused on sorting, classifying, and comparing the physical characteristics of their discoveries. In another example, students from a first-grade class selected an animal that they had observed during a zoo field trip and conducted additional research on their animal, culminating in a presentation to the class the following week. Allowing students to extend their learning from a field trip can maximize the learning potential of the trip and result in an increased conceptual understanding of the science concepts they are learning about (Drapeau 2014).

CHAPTER SEVENTEEN
Flying Monkeys

How do we capture teachable science moments?

At first glance, you might think I have launched into some unexpected *Wizard of Oz* analogies here, but you would be mistaken. There were, in fact, flying monkeys *in my house*. Parents of young children are not likely to be shocked by this; we often find ourselves confronting situations we would have never dreamed of prior to the kiddos entering out lives. So imagine my shock when I walked into the living room, only to be smacked in the face by—you guessed it—a flying monkey. After I recovered from the shock and the jarring impact of the airborne stuffed animal, I realized that there was yet another monkey swinging from the ceiling fan in the middle of the room. I admit to being partly to blame—I may have brought on this whole thing myself by purchasing these long-armed, long-legged monkeys for my little "angels" at a Cubs game the previous year. But when I took a second look at the monkey whirling from the fan, a lightbulb blinked on in my head . . . physics! These monkeys were demonstrating physics right in the heart of our home. So I immediately switched from "mom mode" to scientist and started asking my kids some questions.

"So, guys, this is pretty cool! How did you come up with the idea of hanging the monkeys up there in the first place?" Drew was a little shocked that I was taking so kindly to his mischief but eventually replied, "Well, Mom, we wanted to see how far they would fly when we turned on the fan!" I was immediately intrigued, and we began making guesses about what would happen in different scenarios: "What would happen if you turned the fan on high instead of low?" "How far do you think the monkey would fly if we hung him by his legs, which are longer than his arms?" "What if we slid the monkey farther onto the fan blade?" What ensued was a morning of science, filled with hypothesizing and testing (and a lot of laughing too) with some very engaged children . . . something that certainly would not have happened had I reacted with anger about getting hit in the head with a stuffed animal. I'm certainly not saying I always react this way; there are plenty of times when my kids' mischief has gone too far and resulted in much-needed discipline. But there are also times when it's better to look at our children and their curiosity and decide to "go with it." There are those moments when we have to embrace our children's natural affinity for play and realize that it can lead to some pretty fantastic teachable moments.

And then there are the scary moments. The moments when you find a scorpion in your kitchen sink. Or a frog in your bathroom sink. And I don't even want to talk about the "blender incident." Those moments are a bit trickier for me to embrace, but as a science teacher, I know I just can't miss the opportunity to use every stray creature that finds its way into my house for the greater good. We have observed more creatures than you can imagine in the name of science and have lived to tell about it!

 ## How do we capture teachable moments?

Slow down

What a fast-paced world we live in! There are days when I am so busy that I forget to eat lunch. I experienced tremendous mommy guilt a few weeks ago as I was trying to shuttle my two preschoolers out the door for school. My son was nowhere to be found, and we were running late. Suddenly I spotted him crouched down on the sidewalk, studying a line of ants as they scurried to and from their anthill. I could almost feel my blood pressure rising as I looked at the seconds on the clock ticking. It was then that I said the words that soon caused me the mommy guilt (and science teacher guilt), "We don't have time for this! Get in the car!" Ouch. My heart sank just hearing those words. What would have been the harm in allowing my inquisitive son to observe the ants for thirty seconds? But that's the world we live in, and it is a huge barrier to our ability to capture teachable moments. The same is true in our classrooms. We are under such pressure to meet every standard, get to related arts (specialty classes) on time, make time to cover every content area, and meet the ever-increasing demands of our profession (often without bathroom breaks or a proper lunch). It is no wonder that we just can't afford the time to explore the unexpected teachable moments. But can we really afford to miss them? In my experience, these surprise learning opportunities are often where valuable lessons are learned. This is where conversations occur with those hard-to-reach students. This is where lightbulb moments happen. As hard as it is, we have to try to slow this train down. So when my son wants to track ants at the worst possible time or one of my students asks a really good question just as I'm wrapping up a subject and getting ready to move on to something else, I am challenging myself to take a deep breath and capture the opportunity in front of me before it is gone forever.

Sometimes breaking away from the standards for a minute is OK

Whoa . . . nobody call the standards police. I know this is a major no-no in many schools. As a second-year teacher, I recall being marked down in an evaluation because I strayed from the standards. We were reading a story set in China, and I had *the audacity* to give a little history on the Great Wall of China, which was *not* a grade-level standard. The horror. Obviously we are in agreement on the idea that standards should be the framework for the science that you teach; I preach this to my undergraduates constantly. However, there is a major difference in teaching a unit on something not represented in the standards and doing a quick mini-lesson on a concept that has captivated your students. For example, also during my second year of teaching, we had three major tropical weather systems sweep through our area. Now this might not have been such an issue if we hadn't been in a portable classroom building, surrounded by a field of mud, relying on outdoor portable toilets for our bathroom breaks. But we were. Our primary school's building was in the middle of a major construction project, so we were holding class in a temporary location that proved to be miserable during the flooding. It stands to reason that my students would become fascinated with tracking the tropical weather systems that were giving us a constant soaking. So even though it was not a standard in our grade level, we began to track the tropical systems on a map and learned a little about the weather patterns that were bringing such frequent deluges to our area. After my China incident, I expected the standards police to literally bust through my door and drag me away to wherever they take rebellious teachers like me. But they never came. And my students left a little wiser about some very relevant weather science.

Keep your sense of humor

One of the key elements that has allowed me to keep my sanity during the past decade of my life as a teacher and parent is an active sense of humor. The art of capturing teachable moments actually depends greatly on our own attitude and whether we are going to choose to respond to unexpected (and sometimes unfortunate) situations with laughter or tears. (Anger is a third option, but I find that one even less productive in its teaching potential.) You'll recall that earlier in the chapter I mentioned the "blender incident." You didn't actually think you would escape without us revisiting that one, did you? Of course not.

Well, it all started with such noble intentions. I was in the kitchen attempting to make my own baby food for my six-month-old son. In the absence of a food processor, I had elected to use my blender to puree a batch of steamed carrots (getting hungry yet?). After I had placed the carrots into the blender, my son dropped his pacifier and started to cry, so I ran across the room to pick it up, wipe it off, and hand it back to him. At the same time, the phone rang, and I launched into a complex conversation with my department chair about an upcoming accreditation meeting. I was the very picture of multitasking at its finest (and of sleep deprivation, to be honest); I remember congratulating myself on being the working mom of the century when I made a critical mistake. In the midst of all the chaos in the kitchen, I had forgotten to put the lid on the blender. As I pressed the button to begin the pureeing process, carrots violently exploded out of the blender. It took a minute for me to even realize what was happening. As carrots landed in my hair, all over the counter, on the rug, all over my computer, and even on the baby, I fumbled for the "off" switch. Close to tears, I quickly ended my phone conversation and surveyed the mess. It was then that I saw my carrot-covered child laughing and clapping his hands in the corner; he had certainly kept his sense of humor about the situation. As I began to crack a smile and allow the hilarity of the situation to sink in, I had an idea . . . I was scheduled to teach a session on physics to my undergraduate science majors next week in our science methods class. What could possibly be a better example of Newton's second law of motion (mass, acceleration, and force) than objects flying out of a blender! I am a big believer in using personal experiences that "hook" my students' attention during instruction and also make it more likely that they will remember a specific scientific concept.

So, the next week, I took my undergraduates outside with a blender and the aforementioned carrots. I shared my personal story with them, and we proceeded to make predictions about how far the carrots would travel (acceleration) at different blender speeds (force). We then tested these predictions outside (with safety goggles of course). It turned out to be one of the most memorable lessons I taught that semester, and my students really connected with the concept of Newton's second law of motion. The law states that when the force applied to an object increases, its acceleration increases as well. In this way, the "blender incident" became a teachable moment. What could have easily remained simply an unfortunate kitchen malfunction became an opportunity for teaching a sometimes difficult-to-understand scientific concept. Teachable moments happen every day. If we keep our sense of humor and look at the unexpected occurrences in life with a different lens, we might just discover them.

Appendix A   4Ex2 Instructional Planning Tool: Detailed Organizer

Title of lesson:

Standard:

Objective: observable and measurable

Summative assessment: aligned with objective

Engage: prior knowledge, uncovering student misconceptions, developing a scientific question that can be tested, sparking student interest in a topic

Formative assessments: pre-test, brainstorming, teacher observation, science journals, formative assessments discussed/modeled in class

Explore: giving students the opportunity to explore a concept in science; test a question; experiment

Formative assessments: teacher observation, think-pair-share, science journal, other formative assessment

Explain: helping students make sense of their exploration; guiding them to the main objectives of the lesson; helping connect the exploration to the main ideas of the lesson

Formative assessments: whole-class discussion, small-group discussion, presentations, teacher observation, science journal, rubric

Extend: connecting the main ideas of the lesson to a real-world situation or a different context

Formative assessments: teacher observation, checklist, science journal, rubric, small-group or whole-class discussion

Appendix A 4Ex2 Instructional Planning Tool: Blank Organizer

Title of lesson:

Standard:

Objective:

Summative assessment:

Engage:

Formative assessments:

Explore:

Formative assessments:

Explain:

Formative assessments:

Extend:

Formative assessments:

Appendix A   4Ex2 Instructional Planning Tool: Lesson Template

Title:

Lesson overview:

Standard:

Objective:

Materials:

Procedure:

Engage:

Explore:

Explain:

Extend:

Assessment:

Formative assessments *throughout* the lesson:

Summative assessment to *measure* the lesson objective:

Appendix B   Formative Assessment Examples

> The following examples of formative assessments can be used during the Engage portion of an inquiry-based science lesson to assess students' prior knowledge of a scientific concept. In addition, these formative assessments can be used throughout the lesson as tools to constantly monitor student understanding. Each formative assessment is described within the context of a specific science standard; however, these assessments can be adapted to fit any content area.

Win, Lose, or Draw

Science Context: Illustrating the weather conditions of different seasons

Description of Formative Assessment: This formative assessment allows students to share their prior knowledge in the form of a picture, making it especially appropriate for young children with a limited scientific vocabulary. The teacher prompts the students to "Draw a picture that best illustrates the season of summer." Students then draw their ideas about summer, and the teacher observes the items that are included in their pictures. The teacher continues to ask students to draw their ideas about fall, spring, and winter. Student drawings provide the teacher with information about the students' level of knowledge about the characteristics of each season.

Xs and Os

Science Context: Identifying examples of organisms and nonliving things

Description of Formative Assessment: In this formative assessment, the teacher gives students a list of items and directs them to circle items on the list that are alive and place an "X" beside items on the list that are not alive. Older children may then add a description explaining why they circled the objects they did. For younger children who can't read or write fluently, the teacher can direct a class discussion, asking the students to explain the items they circled. This assessment allows the teacher to assess students' current knowledge of living and nonliving things.

Commit and Toss (Keeley 2008)

Science Context: Describing the function of simple machines

Description of Formative Assessment: The teacher first poses a question to the class. In this case, the teacher may ask, "What type of simple machine can help you lift a heavy object?" The students record their answer on their own piece of paper, crumple the paper into a ball, and throw their paper into the center of the room. Each student then chooses a random piece of paper from the center of the room and reads it to the class, sharing if they agree or disagree with the answer. In this formative assessment, the teacher gains a broad understanding of students' prior knowledge about simple machines and their functions.

Card Sort

Science Context: Classifying animals by physical characteristics

Description of Formative Assessment: Students work either individually or in small groups to sort a set of cards into groups. In this example, students receive a set of twelve cards, each including a picture of an animal.

They then sort the cards into groups of animals that they see as similar. The groups of animals represented in the cards are reptiles, mammals, birds, and amphibians. By viewing the way that students have sorted the cards, the teacher gains an understanding of students' knowledge about animal classifications.

Whiteboards

Science Context: Identifying the needs of living things

Description of Formative Assessment: The teacher organizes students into groups of two or three and gives each group a whiteboard, a marker, and an eraser. The teacher asks the students to draw pictures of what they think animals need to survive. Each group then takes turns sharing their items and explaining their choices. This activity can also be done individually, with each student drawing or writing answers on their own whiteboard. The teacher could choose to have students hold up their whiteboards to quickly take an inventory of each student's answer.

The Hokey Pokey

Science Context: Identifying and classifying plants

Description of Formative Assessment: Most children know the song "The Hokey Pokey," so this formative assessment takes a familiar form. The teacher has the students make a large circle around the room. Then, the teacher makes three to five statements about the topic that the class is studying. For example, the teacher may say, "If you plant a leaf, a tree will grow." Students will "put their right foot in" if they agree with a statement and "put their right foot out" if they disagree. The process repeats again for each round of questions. The teacher may also choose to alter the part of the body used for each round (e.g., This time, put your left elbow in if you agree.)

This assessment makes it easy for the teacher to visually see what his or her students already know or believe.

K-W-L Chart

Science Context: Describing safety precautions for severe weather

Description of Formative Assessment: The teacher gives the students three sticky notes and tells the class that they will be beginning a new unit on severe weather and related safety precautions. On the first Post-it Note, students write something they already **know** about severe weather and safety. On the second Post-it Note, students write something they **want** to learn about severe weather and/or safety. Students then save the final Post-it Note and add something new that they **learn** sometime during the course of the unit. A K-W-L chart is an excellent way to assess what students already know about a topic, gauge areas of student interest, and keep track of what students are learning during the unit.

Red Light/Green Light

Science Context: Identifying the states of matter

Description of Formative Assessment: Red, yellow, and green traffic light icons are used to represent levels of student understanding. Students are given three different-colored cards, asked to assess their own understanding about a concept or skill they are learning, and told to hold up the card that best matches their understanding: green, "I'm doing great and I understand!"; yellow, "I'm doing alright but could use a little help"; and red, "I don't understand and I need help!" These cards can be used at the beginning of the lesson to assess students' current levels of knowledge about solids, liquids, and gases or throughout the lesson to check the pulse of the class periodically.

Four Corners

Science Content: Classifying rocks and minerals

Description of Formative Assessment: For children of the 1980s like myself, this formative assessment brings back memories of a popular game played every weekend at the roller skating rink. In this assessment, the teacher assigns a letter (A, B, C, or D) to each corner of the classroom. The teacher then asks a multiple-choice question, and students walk to the corner that corresponds with their answer. For example, the teacher may ask students to complete this sentence: Igneous rock can be formed by which of the following: A. ocean, B. volcano, C. factory, D. waterfall. Each student then selects an answer and walks to their "corner." This assessment allows the teacher to quickly gauge the current knowledge level of the class while also providing an engaging and social activity for students. When I use this formative assessment with my students, I enjoy listening to students as they try to "justify" their answer and persuade their peers to follow them to their chosen corner. In addition to being an informational tool for the teacher, it's also a great way to get kids talking to each other about science!

Mystery Box

Science Context: Investigating the effects of a push or pull on an object

Description of Formative Assessment: This formative assessment is always a favorite with my students and never fails to capture their attention. The teacher "hides" a clue about the next science unit in a mystery box and students have to ask "yes" and "no" questions to guess the mystery item. For example, in a unit on force and motion, the teacher might use a toy car as the mystery item. Once students guess the item in the box, they get to use this clue to guess what they will be studying next in science. Their guesses reveal a lot about their knowledge of the science connected to the mystery item.

Appendix C Sample Inquiry Lesson for Life Science

Title: Zootopia

Lesson Overview: In this lesson, the students will learn how to classify animals based on their physical features. The students will learn the material and demonstrate their understanding though small-group and whole-class discussion and by completing a matching work sheet.

Standard: Obtain and communicate information to classify animals (such as mammals, birds, amphibians, reptiles, fish, or insects) based on their physical characteristics.

Objective: The student will be able to classify animals based on their physical characteristics with 80 percent accuracy.

Materials: Arrange the following materials and supplies into "exploration stations" as follows:

- assorted pictures of reptiles, amphibians, mammals, and birds
- faux fur (6)
- snakeskin (6)
- plastic bag (6)
- feathers (6)
- mesh (6)
- hard plastic (6)
- magnetic clips
- whiteboard
- matching work sheet
- recording sheet for extend
- pictures of each type of animal on the board
- chart paper
- whiteboard markers
- scratch paper
- pencils

Procedure:

Engage: To begin the lesson, the teacher will show students pictures of three animals (two animals that are similar and one that is different). For example, one group may include lizard, snake, rabbit. Students will be asked which picture out of the three does not fit. The pictures will be labeled one through three reading left to right, and the children will be asked to hold up the number on their fingers that corresponds to a picture on the screen to show which picture does not fit. This allows the children to feel confident when answering and gives the teacher an idea of where the children are in their understanding. After the children hold up the number, the teacher will ask the class to explain why that animal does not fit with the group.

Explore: The teacher will begin by counting off the children into groups of five or six. The groups will then go to a station containing one of six different types of body coverings. The body covering stations will consist of the following: faux fur, snakeskin, a plastic bag with water on it, feathers, mesh, and hard plastic. The students will be allowed one minute to explore and discuss each piece of material before switching to the next material (this means that the students will explore each of the six materials in this way). Once the children have touched and examined each material, they will have five minutes to discuss their thoughts and ask questions within their group. Once the children discuss the objects, the teacher will then point to the pictures on the board (for example, a dog) and then ask the students what material seems most similar to a dog's body covering. The children will decide as a group, write their answer on the piece of scratch paper provided, and take it to the teacher, who will record it on chart paper. Students will go through this procedure for each animal picture on the board (one animal picture for each type of animal skin).

Explain: The teacher will then gather the class together and ask them, "How did you know which material went with each kind of animal?" The teacher and students will then match the correct material from each station to the pictures of the animals on the board. The teacher will tell students the name of each type of animal (reptile, mammal, bird, amphibian). The class will then revisit the pictures of animals from the Engage activity and sort the pictures into the correct group. The teacher will then list physical characteristics for each group. The children will be encouraged throughout the Explain activity to copy the information from the whiteboard into their science notebook.

Extend: If weather permits, students will then practice their skills by going outside and looking for examples of animals from each classification. The information will be recorded on a template prepared by the teacher. The template will contain spaces for students to record animals they observe outdoors. If the children do not observe an animal from each specific group, then the child will be asked to think of an animal that they might see at the zoo and add it to the template.

Assessment:

Formative assessments throughout the lesson: The formative assessments used throughout the lessons are the Engage activity, teacher observation, and small groups for the Explore activity. For the Explain activity, there will be a group discussion to check students' understanding and an outside template for the Extend activity.

Summative assessment to measure the lesson objective: The summative assessment used will be a matching work sheet in which students will match the picture of the animal to the correct name of the animal (reptiles, amphibians, mammals, fish, insects, and birds) along with the correct characteristics of each animal. The assessment will be given to the students at the end of the lesson.

Appendix D   Sample Inquiry Lesson for Physical Science

Title: Ready, Set, Melt!

Lesson Overview: In this lesson, students will learn about the effect that heat has on ice cubes in changing between phases of matter. Students will listen to a book, engage in a small-group discussion, and conduct their own investigations about the effect of heat on ice cubes. Students will make their own predictions and record their observations while working in small groups.

Standard: Conduct structured investigations to test how adding or removing heat can cause changes in solids and liquids.

Objective: The student will be able to successfully conduct an investigation to test how adding heat causes changes in solids.

Materials:

- book (*Amazing Water* by Melvin Berger)
- ice cubes (2 per group)
- paper plates (1 per group)
- Ziploc bags (1 per group)
- timer (2 per group)
- gloves (few pairs)
- paper
- pencils

Procedure:

Engage: The teacher will begin the lesson by reading the book *Amazing Water* by Melvin Berger to introduce the different phases of matter in which water exists. Next, students will share one idea with their neighbor about how they think water might change when it gets hot or cold. The teacher will ask two to three volunteers to share their guesses with the class. The teacher will ask questions such as, "What happens to an ice cream cone when it is out in the sun?" "Why do you think it melts?" The teacher will then inform the class that they are going to be conducting their own investigations using ice cubes to discover how heat affects solids.

Explore: The teacher will begin by giving the students directions. There will be two ice cubes on the desk: one on a plate, and another in a clear plastic bag. There will also be a timer, pencils, and paper for the students to use to record their observations. The class will be divided into groups of four where each student will have a specific job: one timer, two recorders, and one melter. The designated timer will set the timer for ten minutes and be responsible for telling the group when it has been two minutes, four minutes, six minutes, eight minutes, and when time is up. One recorder will observe the ice cube on the plate and draw a picture of what it looks like at each two-minute interval. The other recorder will do the same thing with the ice cube in the plastic bag. The melter will be responsible for holding the ice cube in the plastic bag and working with the recorder so that he can draw a picture of what the ice cube looks like at each interval as well. (The melter may wear gloves if the ice cube is too cold.) Before beginning the investigation, the teacher will ask the students to make predictions about what will happen to the ice cubes. The teacher will also encourage the students to make extra observations about the ice cubes on their paper during the investigation. (e.g., What does it feel like? What shape is it?) Once everyone has made a prediction and is ready to begin, the teacher will have the students begin the timers and start recording their observations.

Explain: After the students have completed their investigations, the teacher will bring them back together in a large group to discuss what happened. The teacher will begin by asking the students, "What happened to the ice cubes?" Other questions the teacher will ask are, "Which ice cube melted faster?" "Why do you think the one you were holding melted faster than the one on the plate?" "Where did the heat come from?" The teacher will then show a short video clip to reinforce the idea that heat has the ability to change a solid to a liquid.

Extend: The teacher will use the interactive whiteboard to create an interactive presentation where students will drag an object to either a warm environment or cold environment depending on where they think the object would change state (i.e., melt or freeze). For example, the board will be divided in half with a beach background on one side and a snowy background on the other. Students will take turns dragging each item to the side of the board where they believe the item will change form (e.g., a student might drag the snowman to the beach side to show that it would melt in the sun because of the heat). The teacher will have five of these scenarios prepared for students.

Assessment

Formative assessment throughout the lesson: The teacher will ask the students questions after reading *Amazing Water* to informally assess their understanding of the book and reveal any prior knowledge the students may have about the phases of matter. Some questions include, "What are phases of matter?" "Can objects (water) change from one state to another?" "What might help water make this change? Temperature?" It will be important to take notes of the students' answers during the discussion to determine which key concepts of the lesson may require extra instruction as well as discover concepts that students may already know to prevent spending unnecessary time on material. During the Explore portion of the lesson, students will be working in small groups. The teacher will walk around the room during this time, make observations, and take notes on students' ideas and interactions.

Summative assessment to measure lesson objective: The teacher will use a rubric as the method of summative assessment for this lesson. Students will receive a score for the following rubric criteria: actively engaged with the group, completed specific role, recorded observations, participated in class discussion.

Appendix E   Sample Inquiry Lesson for Earth Science

Title: Duck and Cover!

Lesson Overview: In this lesson, the students will research tornado safety and precautions to follow when in different locations. Students will discuss, create posters, and present their findings to the class.

Standard: Obtain and communicate information about severe weather conditions to explain why certain safety precautions are necessary.

Objective: The student will be able to explain safety precautions to follow during a tornado at the proficient level.

Materials:

- tornado in the bottle (two 2-liter clear plastic soda bottles, water, tornado tube)
- interactive whiteboard
- poster board (4 sheets)
- crayons
- markers
- construction paper
- computers
- books about tornadoes
- newspaper articles on tornado safety
- magazines on tornado safety
- YouTube video of a tornado
- PowerPoint presentation about tornadoes
- Rubric

Procedure:

Engage: The teacher will create a simulation of a tornado by making a tornado in a bottle. Students will then pass the bottle around and observe the tornado in the bottle. After everyone has seen the tornado, the students will participate in a class discussion. During the discussion, the teacher will record students' answers to the teacher's questions on the interactive whiteboard. The teacher will ask the students three questions: (1) What is happening in the tornado bottle? (2) What do you notice about the water in the bottle? (3) What words do you think of when you hear the word *tornado*?

Explore: Students will work in four groups of five to come up with a tornado plan and safety precautions. The teacher will assign each group one of the following specific locations to study: car, park, mall, or movie theater. The students will have access to books, computers, magazines, and newspaper articles to gather their information about safety in their particular location.

Each group will make a poster illustrating safety precautions, tips, and a picture of the safest place to go to in their location.

Explain: Students will present their findings to the other groups in the class. When all of the presentations have ended, the teacher will ask the students to position themselves in a line in order from the least safe place to be in a tornado to the safest place to be in a tornado. Then the teacher will explain why one location is safer than the others. The teacher will discuss the similarities of the safety precautions. After this activity, the students will go back to their seats. The teacher will show a PowerPoint presentation (created by the teacher) that includes the definition of a tornado and important precautions to remember to be prepared for a tornado.

> Directions on how to assemble the tornado bottle: Fill one of the bottles two-thirds full of water. Take the tornado tube, and twist it on the first bottle. Then, grab the second bottle and attach it to the tornado tube. Turn the tornado maker so that the bottle with the water is on top. Swirl the bottle in a circular motion. In the Northern Hemisphere, most tornadoes form counterclockwise. A tornado will form in the top bottle as the water rushes into the bottom bottle.
>
> If you want to get creative, you can also use food coloring to give the tornado a color and glitter to represent debris.

Extend: The teacher will show a video of a tornado in action. The teacher will make sure the video is appropriate and child friendly. Students will then draw a diagram of their house and write a plan about where they will go if there is a tornado warning while they are at home.

Assessment

Formative assessment throughout the lesson: Formative assessments will include teacher questioning, teacher observation, and group discussion. The teacher will also monitor students during their research and listen to students as they present their posters. Formative assessment will also include a checklist indicating whether students completed a diagram of their house and included necessary tornado safety information.

Summative assessment to measure lesson objective: The teacher will grade students' tornado safety posters with a rubric including the following criteria: explanation of what to do if there is a tornado, a picture identifying the safest place to go for their location, and safety precautions for a tornado.

Appendix F Inquiry-Based Instruction Self-Assessment

Use the following items to assess your own planning and implementation of inquiry-based instruction. (Items adapted from the Electronic Quality of Inquiry Protocol [Marshall, Smart, and Horton 2010])

Components of inquiry-based instruction	Description of proficiency in this component of inquiry	Rating of my own instructional practice in this area 5= very strong area for me 1= very weak area for me
Instructional strategies	Teacher occasionally lectures, but students are usually engaged in activities that help develop conceptual understanding.	
Order of instruction	Teacher asks students to explore before explanation. Teacher *and* students contribute to explanation.	
Teacher role	Teacher frequently acts as facilitator.	
Student role	Students are active learners (involved in discussions, investigations, or activities, but not consistently and clearly focused).	
Knowledge acquisition	Student learning requires application of concepts and process skills in new situations.	
Questioning level	Questioning challenges students up to application or analysis levels.	

Components of inquiry-based instruction	Description of proficiency in this component of inquiry	Rating of my own instructional practice in this area 5= very strong area for me 1= very weak area for me
Complexity of questions	Questions challenge students to explain, reason, and/or justify.	
Questioning ecology	Teacher successfully engages students in open-ended questions, discussions, and/ or investigations.	
Communication pattern	Communication is often conversational with some student questions guiding the discussion.	
Classroom interactions	Teacher or another student often follows up on student responses, encouraging students to justify, apply reasoning, or provide evidence.	
Prior knowledge	Teacher assesses student knowledge and then partially modifies instruction based on this knowledge.	
Conceptual development	Teacher plans activities that require critical thinking.	
Student reflection	Teacher explicitly encourages students to reflect on their learning at an understanding level.	
Assessment type	Formal and informal assessments are used to assess student learning.	
Formative assessment	Teacher solicits explanations from students to assess understanding and then adjusts instruction accordingly.	

Appendix G Sample Science Contracts

Science
Grades Pre-K–1

Safety Rules

1. I will listen carefully.

2. I will follow directions.

3. I will wash my hands after science activities.

4. I will keep myself and others safe.

Safety Contract

I will be a responsible scientist.

_____   _____

Student's signature   Date

_____   _____

Parent's signature   Date

_____   _____

Teacher's signature   Date

Science
Grades 2–3

Safety Rules

Know the class emergency plan.

1. Follow the teacher's written and oral instructions carefully.

2. Ask questions if you do not understand what to do.

3. Do not taste, eat, drink, or inhale anything used in science activities unless the teacher tells you to do so.

4. Keep your hands away from your face, eyes, and mouth during science activities. Wash your hands after science activities.

5. Always wear goggles when chemicals, glass, or heat are being used and when there is a risk of eye injury from flying objects.

6. Tell the teacher if you see something/someone being unsafe.

7. Notify the teacher immediately if you have an accident or an injury, even if the injury is small.

Safety Contract

I have reviewed these safety rules with my teacher and my parent/guardian. I agree to follow these rules and any additional instructions, written or verbal, given by the school and/or teacher.

_____   _____

Student's signature   Date

_____   _____

Parent's signature   Date

_____   _____

Teacher's signature   Date

References

Achieve. 2013. "Next Generation Science Standards." Accessed April 10, 2014.
http://www.nextgenscience.org/.

Bandura, Albert. 1989. "Regulation of Cognitive Processes through Perceived
Self-Efficacy." *Developmental Psychology* 25(5): 729–35.

Black, Paul, Christine Harrison, Clare Lee, Bethan Marshall, and Dylan Wiliam.
2004. "Working Inside the Black Box: Assessment for Learning in the
Classroom." *Phi Delta Kappan* 86(1): 9–21.

Chin, C. 2007. "Teacher Questioning in Science Classrooms: Approaches That
Stimulate Productive Thinking." *Journal of Research in Science Teaching* 44(6):
815–43.

Drapeau, Patti. 2014. *Sparking Student Creativity: Practical Ways to Promote
Innovative Thinking and Problem Solving.* Alexandria, VA: ASCD.

Eccles, Jacquelynne S., and Allan Wigfield. 2002. "Motivational Beliefs, Values, and
Goals." *Annual Review of Psychology* 53: 109–32

Edwards, Carolyn, Lella Gandini, and George Forman, eds. 1993. *The Hundred
Languages of Children: The Reggio Emilia Approach to Early Childhood Education.*
Norwood, NJ: Ablex Publishing.

Fried, Robert L. 2001. *The Passionate Teacher: A Practical Guide.* Boston: Beacon.

Georghiades, Petros. 2004. "From General to the Situated: Three Decades of
Metacognition." *International Journal of Science Education* 26(3): 365–83.

Harris, Christopher J., and Deborah L. Rooks. 2010. "Managing Inquiry-Based
Science: Challenges in Enacting Complex Science Instruction in Elementary
and Middle School Classrooms." *Journal of Science Teacher Education* 21(2):
227–40.

Keeley, Page D. 2008. *Science Formative Assessment: 75 Practical Strategies for Linking Assessment, Instruction and Learning.* Thousand Oaks, CA: Corwin Press.

Kirschner, Paul A., John Sweller, and Richard E. Clark. 2006. "Why Minimal Guidance during Instruction Does Not Work: An Analysis of the Failure of Constructivist, Discovery, Problem-Based, Experiential, and Inquiry-Based Teaching." *Educational Psychologist* 41(2): 75–86.

Kolloffel, Bas, Tessa H. S. Eysink, and Ton de Jong. 2011. "Comparing the Effects of Representational Tools in Collaborative and Individual Inquiry Learning." *International Journal of Computer Supported Collaborative Learning* 6(2): 223–51.

Malaguzzi, Loris. 1993. "No Way. The Hundred Is There." In *The Hundred Languages of Children: The Reggio Emilia Approach to Early Childhood Education,* ed. Carolyn Edwards, Lella Gandini, and George Forman, vi. Norwood, NJ: Ablex Publishing.

Marshall, Jeff C., Bob Horton, and Julie Smart. 2009. "4Ex2 Instructional Model: Uniting Three Learning Constructs to Improve Praxis in Science and Mathematics Classrooms." *Journal of Science Teacher Education* 20(6): 501–16.

Marshall, Jeff C., Julie Smart, and Robert M. Horton. 2010. "The Design and Validation of EQUIP: An Instrument to Assess Inquiry-Based Instruction." *International Journal of Science and Mathematics Education* 8(2): 299–312.

Marshall, Jeff C., and Julie Smart. 2013. "Teachers' Transformation to Inquiry-Based Instructional Practice." *Creative Education* 4(2): 132–42.

Marshall, Jeff C., and Daniel M. Alston. 2014. "Effective, Sustained Inquiry-Based Instruction Promotes Higher Science Proficiency among All Groups: A 5-Year Analysis." *Journal of Science Teacher Education* 25(7), 807–21.

Marzano, Robert J., Debra J. Pickering, and Jane E. Pollock. 2001. *Classroom Instruction That Works: Research-Based Strategies for Increasing Student Achievement.* Alexandria, VA: Pearson.

National Research Council. 2012. *A Framework for K–12 Science Education: Practices, Crosscutting Concepts, and Core Ideas.* Washington, DC: The National Academies Press.

Ormrod, Jeanne Ellis. 2006. *Essentials of Educational Psychology.* Upper Saddle River, NJ: Merrill Prentice Hall.

Rinaldi, Carlina 1998. "Projected Curriculum and Documentation." In *The Hundred Languages of Children: The Reggio Emilia—Advanced Reflections,* ed. Carolyn Edwards, Lella Gandini, and George Forman, 113–25. Greenwich, CT: Ablex Publishing.

Smart, Julie. 2014. "A Mixed Methods Study of Middle School Science Students' Perceptions of Teacher-Student Interactions and Related Domain-Specific Motivation." *Research in Middle Level Education Online* 38(4): 1–19.

Smart, Julie B., and Jeff C. Marshall. 2013. "Interactions between Classroom Discourse, Teacher Questioning, and Student Cognitive Engagement in Middle School Science." *Journal of Science Teacher Education* 24(2): 249–67.

Songer, Nancy Butler, and Amelia Wenk Gotwals. 2012. "Guiding Explanation Construction by Children at the Entry Points of Learning Progressions." *Journal of Research in Science Teaching* 49(2): 141–65.

Tobias, Sigmund, and Howard T. Everson. 2002. *Knowing What You Know and What You Don't: Further Research on Metacognitive Knowledge Monitoring.* New York: College Board.

Tomlinson, Carol Ann. 2014. *The Differentiated Classroom: Responding to the Needs of All Learners,* 2nd ed. Alexandria, VA: ASCD.

Van Zee, Emily H., Marletta Iwasyk, Akiko Kurose, Dorothy Simpson, and Judy Wild. 2001. "Student and Teacher Questioning during Conversations about Science." *Journal of Research in Science Teaching* 38(2): 159–90.

Vygotsky, L. S. 1978. *Mind in Society: The Development of Higher Psychological Processes.* Cambridge: Harvard University Press.

Weiner, Bernard. 2005. "Motivation from an Attribution Perspective and the Social Psychology of Perceived Competence." In *Handbook of Competence and Motivation*, ed. Andrew J. Elliot and Carol S. Dweck, 73–84. New York: Guilford Press.

Wigfield, Allan. 1994. "Expectancy-Value Theory of Achievement Motivation: A Developmental Perspective." *Educational Psychology Review* 6: 49–78.

Wigfield, Allen, and Jacquelynne Eccles. 2002. "The Development of Competence Beliefs, Expectancies for Success, and Achievement Values from Childhood to Adolescence." In *Development of Achievement Motivation.* San Diego: Academic Press, 91–120.

Yin, Yue, Miki K. Tomita, and Richard J. Shavelson. 2014. "Using Formal Embedded Formative Assessment Aligned with Learning Progressions to Promote Conceptual Change in Science." *International Journal of Science Education* 36(4): 531–52.

Index